Blue-Collar God

Blue-Collar
GOD

Terry Esau

W PUBLISHING GROUP™
www.wpublishinggroup.com

A Division of Thomas Nelson, Inc.
www.ThomasNelson.com

Published by W Publishing Group, a Division of Thomas Nelson, Inc., P.O. Box 141000, Nashville, Tennessee, 37214.

Library of Congress Cataloging-in-Publication Data available

Esau, Terry, 1954–
    Blue collar God/white collar God / by Terry Esau.
        p. cm.
    ISBN 0-8499-1704-2
    1. Christian fiction, American. I. Title.

PS3605.S73 B58 2001
813'.6—dc21   2001045579

Printed in the United States of America
02 03 04 05 BVG 9 8 7 6 5 4 3

To Mary and our three girls,
Brianna, Lauren, and Taylor.

What would my life be without this twisty-turny
roller-coaster adventure we're on? And who
would I be without the four of you, wide-eyed
and screaming with life? Thanks for making every
day a thrill ride. I love you guys. Keep your hands
up, here comes a big one!

Acknowledgments

To my family, the whole Esau gang—we didn't live in a mansion, but I learned early on that mansions are sometimes tucked in the walls of unassuming homes. Love creates a wealth that can't always be seen from the outside. Even though we didn't know it at the time, we were rich. My brother, my sisters, and I are still cashing in on the dividends of our heritage. I'm grateful.

To my wife's family, the Soholts—boy, did I get lucky. Not only did I get the girl of my dreams, but a matched set of beautiful people, inside and out.

To Joey, Laura, David, Mark, Lanie, Rob, Laurie, Tom, Christina, and all the people at W Publishing Group— thanks for believing and betting on a long shot.

Thanks, Neal, for walking my manuscript into Joey's office. You're the best non-agent I've ever not hired.

Lela Gilbert, my editor—when I mentioned thanking her in my acknowledgments she simply said, "You're welcome. There, I've been sufficiently thanked." Not so quick there, little missy. We connected from day one . . . message, style, and personality. I'm not sure if that's a compliment or not, but I've enjoyed the process, and I appreciate your imprint on this book.

Woodridge Church—where I regularly get my cup refilled with his special concoction. This book is a thermos of sorts, sent out from all of you.

The Lake Country Coffee gang—the Steinhafels, Ericksons, Pollacks, Nords, and Hilbelinks . . . see you Sunday.

Steve, Jerry, Dan, and Kevin—college buddies that morphed into lifelong friends. Keith and Van—guys as crazy as me, which explains why we're so close. Bob and Tom, my obsessed cycling buddies—"Speed and Pain," you gotta love those ugly twins!

My tenth-grade guys group—wish I would've been half that cool at sixteen.

Varen Herman, Kevin Meyer, Paul Johnson, Bob Jr., R.B., Dave Whiting, D.K., Rick Barron, Brad and Donna,

Wolfies, Wessners, John Olson, John Vawter, Dick Wilson, Steve Gottry, Maxine Posegate, Judith Guest, the Great Adventure class, all of Dickey Lake Drive, Mountain Lake (the "Little City with Big Ideas"), and the entire roster of the Esau Christmas card list—you've all tweaked my life in one way or another. You've all been guinea pigs of sorts. Thanks.

To my wife, Mary, and our girls (see "Dedication" and "Home")—to say any more would have to be categorized as excessive gushing.

To you, the readers—thanks for shelling out a few bucks to read the ramblings of an ex–advertising guy. I spent a bunch of years marketing products I didn't really care about, and now, finally, I'm pitching something I believe in. And, let me tell you, I couldn't be having more fun! I hope you fall in love with this product.

Blue Collar Contents

Blue-Collar God

He could have been born the son of a CEO. He could have attended a snooty prep school. He could have shuffled himself into the deck of humanity as a king.

But he didn't.

He came as a three of clubs.

He chose to be common. Ordinary. Regular.

He was born in a blue-collar hospital. He lived a blue-collar life. He hired a blue-collar crew and ran a blue-collar ministry. He was, literally, one of us.

In *Blue-Collar God,* that's exactly how I hope to portray him. Approachable. Accessible. I want to bring him down to the level to which he willingly brought himself; down to earth, down to us. He pressed the button for the basement of existence, becoming sub-God, trading in his puncture-resistance for human flesh.

Imagine . . .

> God, a New York City cabdriver.
> God, a garbageman.
> God, a kite maker.
> God, a homeless insurance salesman.
> The I Am, now Everyman.

These are the stories of a God who gave up his CEO position to become a grunt, who traded his high-profile I Am status for a lowly John Doe existence. Instead of us struggling to live up to God, he willingly chose to live down to us. These are the stories of a God who went to great lengths to erase the disconnectedness between us and him.

This book is for people who struggle with that disconnectedness, who struggle to feel a closeness with God, who struggle walking with him even though they may be working for him. It's for people who have accepted God's gift of grace but have left it sitting under the tree, unwrapped. It's for people who keep asking for his forgiveness but are suspicious as to whether it has been granted. This book is for kitelike people who keep trying to fly themselves with no strings attached.

These stories aren't all neat and tidy. They're pictures of real life and the things that sometimes happen in real life. The symbolism may disturb you at times, but stick with me, follow the images all the way through and reach for the underlying nugget of truth. My wish is not to offend, but to jump-start our thought processes by sketching some pictures of God that are a bit nontraditional. After all, a God who swapped deity for humanity, even if only for a while, can't be accused of being overly traditional.

My hope is that you will become more comfortable with this nontraditional God who became human, ordinary; that you will feel a safeness in reaching for his calloused hand, that you will become more trusting of a God who willingly traded his white-collar superiority for blue-collar accessibility. These are the stories of a God who became a regular guy. A God who became approachable, accessible—blue-collar.

The Fitting Room

So you want to try on a shirt? Good. I see you've got one of the preworn denim shirts there . . . the blue-collar variety. That's my choice too. They're so comfortable. No pretension, no starchy attitude. They're real—I like that.

Why don't you go first. In fact, there are about ten rugged work shirts on the shelves of the following pages . . . try 'em all on. I'll wait. I've got a feeling once you slip one of these babies on you'll be as hooked as I am.

These aren't just your average jean shirts you know. They've made some pretty wild claims. Like, "Sure, we'll make you look better on the outside, but we'll dress you up inside too." I know, it sounds a little far-fetched, but I'm giving it a shot. It's gotta be some kind of supernatural fabric . . . God cloth or something.

Go ahead. I can't wait to see what it looks like on you.

Oh, and when you're done here, head over to the White Fitting Room if you haven't already done so. They've got some very chic white dress shirts over there—the white-collar variety. I have a feeling they're going to knock you out; check out the whole rack. After you've tried all of them on, meet me back here and we'll wear our new shirts home. We'll surprise everyone with our new look, the new us.

If you need any other sizes, just yell.

Hip-Pocket God

This morning I was KO'd by reality. Took a hard left to the jaw. Never even saw it coming.

Well, let me back up a little and tell the whole story . . .

A few years back I found God. Or maybe I should say he found me. Anyhow, we latched onto one another—for good.

Once I found him, that was it. I never wanted to be without him again. So, I stuck him in my pocket. Stuffed him way down deep in the right front pocket of my Levi's button-fly jeans. Whenever I needed him I just reached into the pocket of my 501s and there he was.

It was great to have him there. Instant access. Instant friend. Less than a phone call away. It made me feel good, secure.

I used to haul him out of my pocket for no reason at all.

Just to see him, to be with him. Sometimes I'd even pull him out at parties so my friends could see him. It was fun. God, the ultimate party favor.

Well, a couple of years passed, I got married, a kid on the way, bought a house—you know, started living that American dream thing.

Business got busy.

Bills grew bigger.

One day I noticed that my right front pocket was getting pretty crowded—cash, credit cards, keys, and all. So I decided to move God to my left front pocket. After all, he was still right there. Still accessible. Still my friend.

Now it was a lot easier to get at my money. Just reach in and there it was. No obstruction. Nothing in the way. I felt a little freer with it, too, now that I didn't have to go around God to get at it. But, hey, it was my money so what's the big deal?

Life progressed. Our baby was born. A beautiful baby girl . . . we named her Bailey. I loved that kid, more than anything in the world. But now we needed a bigger house, more room, more furniture—better furniture. I got a boat. Didn't have much time to use it, but I had it. Had to work more to pay for it all. My schedule was getting crazy. I made endless to-do lists and crammed them into my left front pocket till the seams were about to burst.

That pocket was getting too full to hold all of my activities . . . and God. Something had to change. After all, there were only twenty-four hours in a day.

I couldn't really cut back on work. I had bills to pay.

I couldn't give less time to my family. They were already getting the short end of the stick.

How uncomfortable could my right hip pocket be, anyway? I thought.

He seemed to accept the move without putting up too much of a fuss. And why should he? What difference would it make to God? He was still accessible. Still within reach. Still my friend—occasionally.

I guess I didn't pull him out at parties anymore. It would have been uncomfortable, contrived. We seemed to have more of a business-type relationship now. One of respect, a formal regard. But hey, I grew up. And so did my God. I still pulled him out sometimes . . . if I needed him.

Again, time marched on. Bailey continued to toddle her way into my heart. She called me Dabby. Man, I loved that kid. But her mother and I were having problems. Little hurdles had become concrete walls. Indifference had become spite. Lukewarm, now stone cold.

Loneliness sank deeper and deeper into my right hip pocket.

I thought I found some of that warmth again in another woman. Someone from work. Someone to take the edge off of my loneliness. We added some heat all right. But warmth? Not really. The fuse was short and the warmth was long gone before I got home to kiss my sleeping Bailey good night.

I tucked my little affair as deep down as I could get her in my right hip pocket hoping she'd stay, quiet as a church mouse. Our sacred little secret. But as I was pulling my hand out of my pocket, I brushed—the back of my hand touched— the face of God. A chill raced up the skin of my arm. What was I doing? What kind of an idiot was I? I couldn't bury my little affair and God in the same pocket. I couldn't confine my fantasy next to his purity. Even I knew that.

I quickly reached in, ashamed to even look his way, and I practically threw God from my right to my left hip pocket with one swooping motion.

There. That's done. I half expected God to protest this move, but again, he didn't. Of course, I didn't pull him out to ask him how he felt about it, either. I would have had to look him in the eye to do that. I didn't dare.

God didn't see the light of day too often after that. My pocket became his prison. For the most part, I forgot he was even in there. What was a business relationship became a forgotten acquaintance. Like a classmate from first grade that you can hardly remember even when you look at the old pictures. God had become a nonentity.

And life dragged on.

Then one day I bought a new pair of jeans, and I forgot to transfer God from the hip pocket of my old jeans to my new ones. I never even thought about it—I mean him.

Then, like I was saying, one morning reality caught me on the chin. My little girl, my Bailey, was hit by a car. She was just playing in the front yard, innocently. I suppose a ball went into the street or something. She just ran after it.

The doctor said the surgery went well, whatever that means.

While she was in the operating room, I felt as if my heart was being dissected. I needed God like I had never needed him before. Instinctively I reached my hand into my right front pocket.

But he wasn't there. I tried my other pocket.

No God.

I desperately reached around for my back pockets.

Two hip pockets—no God.

I glanced around the room and felt it closing in on me. Panic set in. I lost it.

"Where are you, God?" I screamed at him. "You're supposed to always be with me, never forsake me. Don't you care? What good are you if you disappear when I need you the most? Talk to me, God!"

The silence crushed me.

I cried from the basement of my soul. For the first time in my life I realized that all of my pockets were empty. Without God my work was meaningless.

My money, useless.

Life, lifeless.

I walked into Bailey's room. She was still unconscious. I sat across from her, staring with a helplessness that ached beyond words. Her little clothes were folded and sitting on an end table beside me . . . blood splotches, witnesses to the tragedy. I ran my hand across her little jeans, hoping to feel the memory of life. I slid my hand into her right front pocket, out of curiosity, wondering what priceless treasure my little baby had been collecting this fateful day.

Then I lost my breath. There in her pocket was God. Her God and my God. The God of her present and the God of my past. His eyes held no judgment, only tears for the pain of my little Bailey. Our little Bailey.

He looked at me with a father's love and said, "I love that kid too."

He found me again, today. Or should I say I found him, in the right front pocket of my Bailey's 501 jeans.

The Shirt Tale

Allow me to introduce myself. I'm the future of fashion, haute couture, style with a big fat *S*. People see me coming and they say, "Look out, here comes Mr. Cool." Armani, ha! Versace, I don't think so. Gucci? He wishes he was me. No—I'm the one and only . . .

The Dirty Blue Leisure Suit.

I've always been different—from the very beginning. I'm what you would call an overachiever, never satisfied. If there's a higher shelf in the closet, this Leisure Suit's moving up. And you better stay outta my way or I'll wrinkle your scrawny fingers. I just don't care. Let me put it this way—you mean nothing to me . . . less than nothing. Got it?

You're looking at my fabric, aren't you? It's undestandable, everybody does. My piece goods are top-shelf; of course it's a little hard to tell through all this . . . aromatic film. I'm so coated with dirt, grease, and grime that my threads are practically organic. Ask me if I care. No! I'm toxic and I'm proud. Deal with it.

I haven't always looked like this. When I came off the table I was a whole different shade of magnificent. Even my designers said so. I was the best thing they'd ever done. I was the pinnacle of the fashion industry . . . well, almost. You see, there were these three guys who created me—The Suit, The Shirt, and The Tie. They were the top, the zenith, no one looked like them. They turned heads, they caught eyes—not just some, everyone's. They were "The Look." They had a flair the rest of us could only dream about.

That was my problem, I was a dreamer. I spent hours alone in front of the mirror, trying to make myself look like them. I pretended to be them, I acted like them. I tried to become them. Why couldn't I be The Look? Why couldn't I rule the fashion industry? After all, I was the Blue Leisure Suit!

Well, they didn't see it that way. The Suit, The Shirt, and The Tie—they stripped me off my hanger, they threw me on the floor. They banished me from their closet, forever.

Now, I have to spend my days slithering around, soaking up every drop of oily sludge that touches me. I'm so slippery I can't even stay on a hanger anymore; I just slide off. I hate The Look.

Yeah, I fell a long way, but like I said, I'm an over-achiever. I wasn't done yet, not by a long shot. I had a plan up my sleeve to unravel The Look, thread by exquisite thread; and I knew exactly how to hurt them.

You see, they had designed a whole new line of shirts, a separate closet filled with them. They were tailored after the original Shirt, but without his fabric. They were just cotton . . . nothing special at all. But The Look was gaga over these shirts. The Look thought they were the coolest thing ever. They were so attached to these shirts it was like they were sewn together or something. I didn't get it, but that one weakness—that unnatural affection—that was the flaw I needed to rip The Look apart at the seams.

One day Yours Truly wormed his way into the shirt closet. This was going to be fun. I had showered in a pint of Old Spice to cover up the smell of the oil slick that ran down the middle of my spine. I turned the charm meter up to eleven. I crouched on the shelf, 10W-30 venom dripping from my lapels. I slithered up to the shirts and started seducing them with questions like, "Wow, you guys look good. I wonder what you'd look like with a—a tie around your neck?" Or, "I can just picture you guys in Armani smoking jackets." I told them, "The Look doesn't leave the closet half dressed, why should you?"

I can be pretty persuasive.

Then I slid to the edge of the shelf, turned my rumply padded shoulders a bit and said, "Come on, fellas, every shirt deserves a jacket. You can be more than just shirts. You can be suits—just like The Look." Then I spread my jacket wide open to them and said, "Hey, tell you what, I'll show you what you'd look like if you were part of a suit." I leaned my mirror up against the wall so they could see themselves and then I said, "Come here. Try me on. Go ahead, throw me over your shoulders. I won't bite."

It was a slick sales pitch. Smooth as ice.

They slipped.

Every last one of them. Shirt after shirt they slid into my 42-Regular cavity. I hung all over them like an abscess. They might have gotten a momentary buzz, a flash of—coolness—but as they took me off, the only thing they were left with was dirt. Grime. Slime. I grew on them like a fungus.

The Suit, The Shirt, and The Tie were devastated. This was the first time I had ever seen this trio of fashion mavens look a bit disheveled. It was unbelievable. I had done it. I had polluted their little breed of tagalongs so thoroughly that they couldn't even stand to be near them. Their preppy little collection of button-down Oxfords had fallen under my spell. Now, instead of them resembling the original Shirt, they clashed—like pink and red. They looked more like me now. They looked like hell, and I loved it. I finally had my own line. I owned them, I ruled them. They were—mine.

And The Look left.

Things were going well in my little closet kingdom. I had a vast wardrobe to sully and smear, and I did my best to decorate them all with my toxic touch. I doused them with my essence, making it clear that they were mine to wear and tear as I wished.

Then, one day I noticed there was a new shirt on the rack. It arrived inconspicuously, practically snuck into the closet through the barn door, unnoticed. I knew who it was right away. It was The Shirt. But something was different about him, a lot different.

First off, I'd never seen him without The Suit and The Tie before. I'm not sure if they'd ever been separated. He looked naked, exposed. He looked ordinary. Where were his glowing buttons, his crisp collar, his triple stitching, his fabrique par excellence? Gone. Now he was made of cotton—plain old grown-in-the-ground cotton—just like his generic blue-collar pals.

What was he doing here? What was he up to? Where were his little buddies, The Suit and The Tie? This whole scenario made me a little edgy.

He started chumming around with the shirts, and they got to know him—in a different way than they had known him before. He told them how they each contained several threads from the original Shirt, how they were designed by The Suit and The Tie, how they were adored. Blah, blah, blah. I could tell they didn't understand much of it, but they soaked up what they could. And the more of him they soaked up, the less of me they were absorbing.

At first I was cautious, thinking any day The Suit and The Tie would show up and I'd have to scurry off to the floor. But they never did. Day after day they left that vulnerable Shirt to fend for himself. Their absence gave me the courage to become a tad more enterprising.

I met up with him one day. I invited him to try me on, promising all kinds of things I knew I couldn't deliver. He just stared at me like I was some freak of fashion. I hate that. Especially since his fabrique mystique had degenerated into the look-and-feel-of-cotton. Who did he think he was? I had a feeling the two of us were headed for a showdown.

I like showdowns where the odds are stacked in my favor, so I started plotting an elaborate scheme to rip him to shreds. The plan was to start with small rips, insignificant tears . . . to fray him a little here and there, and then, eventually, turn him into a tidy little box of rags.

My plan was working like a charm. I got most of the closet to start picking at him, scrutinizing him. They started to think of him as a radical. The very thing he claimed to be was the last thing they thought he was. Somehow I convinced them he was a fraud. Ironic, isn't it?

They actually started to hate him. I was so proud of my stupid little shirts. They wanted to kill him even more than I did. It's funny—he made the same mistake again—he overestimated these shirts. Love is a miscalculation of fools. Trust is the seedling of betrayal. I can't believe he couldn't see that.

Well that frail fool was betrayed all right . . . right into my hands. And I was ready for him. I had the perfect hanger picked out. It was one of those big fat wooden ones, jagged and splintered, eager to snag anything that came close. They draped him on that thing. They hung him out to dry. They did things to him I'm not sure I would have had the guts to do.

Then I saw something I thought I'd never see. I saw a

little grease spot appear on his collar. Not big, but it was visible. It was definitely a grease spot. Then I saw another speck materialize on the front of The Shirt. Then the smudges started coming faster and faster. It was a hailstorm of garbage rocketing toward The Shirt. All the stink and grime in the closet became like asteroids, propelled, swallowed by the black hole on the hanger. I don't know if it was magnetic or gravitational . . . or supernatural . . . but somehow, someway he was single-handedly sanitizing every shirt in the closet. He had become the target for every contaminant, every pollutant. He was inhaling everything I had ever coughed up.

Even though I hated seeing the shirts get cleaned, it was a barter I gladly welcomed just to see him filthy. They could be had again, but him, who knows. I was enjoying this moment.

This was too good to be true. He was just hanging there, drenched in slime. Now his fabric was indiscernible. He was more crud than cloth. More torn than whole. The added weight of the sludge caused the splinters to tear more deeply into his fabric. He was rapidly coming apart at the seams.

Then, he looked at me, almost like he was inviting me to finish him off. I couldn't believe what a fool he was. He was playing himself right into my hands. I was giddy with excitement. This was my fantasy, the moment I'd dreamed about over and over. And here it was—here he was, just a few threads away from tumbling to hell. There wasn't much holding him to the hanger now. I was hyperventilating, but I waited. This was my chance. Still, I waited. Then, it was time, my time.

Now!

I lunged over the edge of the shelf, and as I plummeted past The Shirt I reached out and wrapped my sleeves around his torso, wrenching him from the hanger. He tore. His fabric exploded. He was unraveling right before my eyes. I screamed with delight as we fell. Down, down we flew.

"Welcome to my home!" I shrieked as we splashed into a brackish pool of slime. Wave after wave, we were doused, tossed, and tumbled in a deluge of greasy gruel. It was a tsunami of filth. I could have happily drowned in it.

Finally, I pulled myself off of him. He lay there, still, motionless. I leaned in, squinting, listening.

Nothing.

I poked him with my lapels.

Nothing.

"Get up, Shirt!" I said, stepping on his neck.

Nothing.

"Ha!" I danced on his carcass. I stood over him cackling like a crowned crow—laughing, dripping, drooling. It was the greatest moment of my life.

I watched him shrivel up into a ball as he was swallowed by the pool of noxious waste. I watched him sink. I watched him disappear.

I watched him . . . die.

But that's not the end of the story.

Not even close. I should have known better. After all, he's The Shirt. And he happens to know The Suit and The Tie, personally. It seems they had a plan up their sleeves too—well, The Suit did at least.

I heard this distant sound, like a trumpet. That's right, the cavalry was coming. The Suit and The Tie decided to go closet-hopping, looking for that certain Shirt to complete their outfit. They came to rescue him. The Tie, hanging from the pocket of The Suit, stretched all the way to my smelly little corner of the closet, plunged into the creosote puddle, and grabbed on to his collar. Then, with one enormous tug, they jerked The Shirt from my grasp. The Suit and The Tie yanked him with such force that every microscopic spec of grime was ripped from his threads and splattered back down on me like a tidal wave of gutter goo from Jiffy Lube.

As I looked up through the fog, struggling to focus, I couldn't believe what I was seeing. The Shirt—he was new again. He was clean. Except for a few patches, he looked immaculate . . . and his buttons, they were glowing, and his fabric . . . well it wasn't cotton anymore, that's for sure.

He was back.

I slithered as far down into the corner as I could get. I was scared, shattered. What was left for me? What was left of me? Now what?

I'll tell you what. I dropped four sizes. I atrophied to a 38 Slim. Nothing has been the same since then. My dirt won't even stick to the shirts anymore. It's like he Scotch-garded them or something . . . they just look at him and the dirt falls off. Do you know how frustrating that is?

The only good news for me in all this is that The Look decided to head back to their own closet, that palatial walk-in closet in the sky. They've got big plans to bring this whole line of shirts up there someday . . . have an eternal fashion show with gold runways and all. Big deal.

For now, they're leaving the shirts in my . . . care. Ha! Well, almost. The Tie—I hate The Tie—he decided to stay here. That satiny little twerp spends his days sashaying around the closet, hanging on everyone's neck, reminding them that they're cool, that they're washable, that they're knockoffs from the original Shirt. He's got them convinced that they're something special, just because The Shirt said so, just because he "saved" them. I don't know. Maybe they are.

I hate The Shirt.

I hate The Shirt.

I hate The Shirt.

It's not fair. Just when I thought I had crushed The Shirt, The Shirt crushed me. Oh, I'm still here. I'm not officially dead, but I'm dead—I'm as good as dead. The end of the story has already been written, and I'm way dead. Sure, I'm still hanging around the floor of the closet, still looking to mess up anything I can, but it's just a matter of time before I'm—

. . . dead.

I'm dead.

Christoholics Anonymous

"*Hi. My name is Peter,* and I'm a . . . Christoholic."

"Hi, Peter!"

I was sweating 45-caliber bullets by the clip-full. This was my first CA meeting. My brother, Andy, had somehow convinced me to come. Now, with my knees a'knockin', I felt like pistol-whipping him for talking me into this nonsense.

As I looked around the room, assessing my predicament, I wondered, *Who are these people?* They seemed friendly enough . . . certainly gave me a rousing "Hi, Peter," but who were they—really? Jesus freaks? A Christian cavalry? A convention of pious pocket protectors?

I had to admit, they were outwardly unimpressive, seriously average. A pardon-me-for-almost-living clan of codependent dependents. Cowering zealots, sniveling saints. Oh, they believed in *Christ,* all right, but they were determined to keep that belief *anonymous.*

As I looked over this haggard herd, I began to wonder what had possessed me to want to wear their brand. Then I remembered why I had consented to come.

I, too, was a spiritual chicken.

My faith had become an embarrassment to me. A real burden. A hassle. It was the part of me I wished to keep anonymous. These people understood that and empathized with me.

It's so tough being a Christian these days. Friends make fun of us, science lambastes our beliefs, and the media crucify our convictions. Hanging on to our inner tubes of faith is exhausting. Sometimes I'm not sure if *it's* keeping *me* afloat or vice versa.

So this was to be my new support group. Friends in the faith. Cohorts in Christianity. It seemed more like pablum religion for placebo believers . . . hanging on to our mediocre faith by our fingernails.

It wasn't always this way. I understand Christoholics used to be a real live-wire bunch . . . borderline radicals. Encouraging fellow believers to live with reckless abandon.

Testing the outer limits of faith. Blabbing their convictions to anyone who would listen, a real devil-may-care attitude.

But that was a different time, and somewhere along the line things changed. This bubbling cauldron of faith-a-nat-ics had cooled to the safe thermal state of born-again bath-water—no longer hot enough to disinfect, nor cool enough to refresh. They had been rendered harmless, useless. Ineffectual. Congregating in dark rooms with latched doors. They leaned against one another like frail, plucked flowers—parched, desperate for water. And now, here I was joining this blah bouquet.

Without much passion, I started my spiel: "Like I said, I'm Peter, and sometimes I'm embarrassed to be a Christian." The empathetic allies moaned with understanding. "Yesterday I was at work and my coworkers were telling some pretty risqué jokes . . . just having a good time, when one of them looks at me and mockingly says, 'Oh, sorry, Peter. I forgot you're a *Christian*. I didn't mean to embarrass you.'"

"I told them it was no problem, that I wasn't *that kind* of Christian. Oh, I was embarrassed all right. But not because of the jokes. I can deal with that. What bugs me is how they treat me like I'm different, you know, like a—a Christian. I hate that! Sometimes I wish I'd never heard of Jesus!"

That flare lit up the room. Sure, they'd all thought the

same thing, but this group was generally not willing to bare their feelings quite that honestly.

"Thanks for sharing with us, Peter." Tom, the president of our little club of balking believers, patted me on the back as I left the stage. "We all know how uncomfortable it is to stand out in a crowd."

The patronizing attitude repulsed me. Why did I need these people? Why couldn't I just live the Christian life like I knew it was meant to be lived . . . or else just blow the whole thing off. Forget it. This living in the middle—this no man's land—this sacred clean room—was pure bull!

Well, the meeting dragged on. We'd already recited the Christoholics Anonymous Motto together: "Everything in moderation—especially Jesus." We'd done the secret hand-shake, which was never employed outside this room, and we'd sung the theme song, "Love Isn't Love Till You Give It Away."

We'd covered old business: membership drive, dues, parking permits . . .

New business: door prizes, adding a thirteenth step to our Twelve Step program. ("Every smile is a prayer, every raindrop a blessing." I'm not sure what the heck that means, but they all seemed pretty psyched about it.)

Tom, our languid leader, was about to wrap up the

festivities when he was interrupted by a man walking in from the back. This man proceeded all the way down the aisle till he stopped right in front of the podium.

Tom, unable to continue with the man standing smack-dab in his face, asked, "Excuse me, sir, may I help you?"

The man spoke, "Well, I was wondering if I might be able to join your group?"

"Are you a believer?" asked Tom, a twinge of excitement over the prospect of a new recruit . . . more dues for the coffers.

"Yes, I am."

"Then I don't see why not. Come on up here and introduce yourself."

The man walked up the four stairs and pulled alongside the president. "Why don't you tell us your name and occupation," said Tom.

"My name is Jesus Christ—and, my occupation, uh, well, I guess I'm the Savior of the . . . the world." He delivered the line without pretense.

All sound vanished, as if it had been sucked through the air vents by an industrial-strength audio ShopVac. Heads turned. Brows furrowed. One guy, assuming this to be a left-over April Fools' Day prank, sang out the typical response to all intros at CA, "Hi, Jesus!"

Jesus smiled and said, "Hi, Greg." When Greg realized that there was no way this guy could have read his "Hello, My Name Is Greg" name tag from fifty feet, his facial pigment fled, leaving him with a birch-bark complexion.

I will admit, he got my attention too.

Jesus, recognizing the black hole in leadership, decided to proceed. "I was just wondering if I could join your group? You know, come to your meetings, hang out with you all? I'm kind of a Christoholic myself, you know."

Tom, scooping his jaw from the podium, corralled a couple of wayward words clanging around in his cranium. "Uh, OK. Sure."

For some reason I felt this surge of courage, like the irrational boldness of a self-confident drunk. Prompted by a curiosity to find out what was really going on here, I stood and asked, "Excuse me, um, Jesus, but why would you want to join this group? After all, we're all paranoid that people will find out that we believe in you. We're not exactly your most ardent supporters."

"I know that." Jesus looked at me tenderly. "I will admit, I was tempted to give you all legionnaires' disease, but then I settled down and realized that even a mustard seed of faith can grow. And yours will, too, if you get to know me."

"Get to know you?"

"Yeah. Spend time with me. Talk to me. Listen to me. We'll become good friends. And when you really know who I am, you won't be embarrassed by me anymore. I think you'll be proud to be associated with me, as I am with you."

It was interesting to think we'd been embarrassed to be seen as his followers, while he seemed perfectly comfortable locking arms with cockroaches like us.

Jesus continued, "What do you think? Does that sound like something you'd be interested in?"

I was ready to jump. Impulsive reactions had always ruled me and I wasn't about to change now. Following my gut, I said, "I would!" I said it and I meant it. A few others chimed in. "Yeah. Me too."

The vast majority, however, mentally weighed the cost of this invitation, ran the numbers, and decided the share price was too high. The investment too great. They got up and shuffled out, eyes at half-mast. Tom, our doubting leader, led the exodus.

When the dust had settled, what remained was still unimpressive. Still cowardly. Still a band of ragtag stragglers with dwarfed faith. And now, far fewer in number. A meager twelve.

But, everything else had changed. Now we had a real

leader again. The right leader. It was like we were going back to our roots, back to our first love . . .

Jesus.

And we were looking at him—looking to him for direction, purpose, and meaning. Something told me my world was about to be turned upside down, and I was looking forward to it.

Jesus' eyes sized up this handful of anonymous Christoholics. Half to himself, he said, "Twelve. Hmm." Then looking at me he said, "Well, Peter, you rock, I guess we can change the world with twelve. Don't you think?"

And so we did.

Garbageman God

I was looking through the Yellow Pages for a new garbage removal service. It's not that my old one wasn't doing an adequate job, but there was the occasional piece of trash left on the driveway, no holiday service, and punctuality—I believe he put it this way, "I'll gets to it when I gets to it." Seems like the raccoons often got to it before he did.

So how do you pick a new garbageman? The fanciest ad? The one with the largest and newest fleet of trucks? The environmentally responsible refuseologist?

The one that caught my eye simply read, "God's Garbage Removal. You carry it, we bury it!" Seemed simple enough. The "God" thing threw me a little, but hey, everybody's got to have an angle.

What I wasn't prepared for was the thoroughness of God's garbage plan. He called it his "Theory of Trash."

"Everybody's got it," he said. "It doesn't matter how hard you try, you're gonna end up with all kinds of rubbish. And when something goes bad you want to get rid of it right away, get it out of the house. If there's one thing I know, it's that you can't live forever with trash in your house. No, sir." The way he said it I sensed he had an unnatural dislike for trash, almost a hatred. Which of course made me wonder why he was in the business.

He continued, "So, I can pick up once a day, twice a day, once a week, whatever you'd like. You can call me twenty-four hours a day and I'll come right over—be there in thirty minutes or less. If it takes me longer, the pickup is free. Heh, heh, heh." He chuckled at his own folksy joke.

I'll admit, I was impressed by his dedication to service, so I booked him. Once a week. Seemed about right.

"How about Thursday mornings, say, around 9:30?"

"Perfect," he said. "I'll be there."

And he was. Took away every tidbit of junk. Right down to the last tissue. Not a trace of garbage left. I noticed that he even brought my garbage cans back up to the garage. It's like he was encouraging me to start filling them again, immediately.

It felt good to be debris free. Clean.

The next week I met him at the curb. You know, a little small talk with the drayman. "So, uh God, where do you take this stuff? Is there a landfill around here somewhere?"

"Oh no. I haul this pile of filth to the other end of eternity. Heh, heh. As far as the east is from the west, you know. Don't worry; you won't smell this stuff again, ever. Heh, heh, heh." For somebody who hated trash he sure seemed to love his work.

One day I saw him out by the curb, washing the driveway. Scrubbing the asphalt where the trash had been sitting. Every single trace of trash—gone. Sanitized. Purified. It was almost like the trash had never existed. Talk about a neat freak.

One Thursday I was in an unusually ornery mood, just plain ticked off. I was more in a state of mind to wallow in my trash than haul it. It happens sometimes. Besides, I figured with an overzealous garbageman like God, he'd probably come get it right out of my garage. Shoot, he'd probably come gather it from my counters, bag it, schlep it, the whole nine yards.

I was still in bed when I heard his truck pull up. I heard the engine idling. I waited to hear him pull away but he never did. A half-hour later he was still there. Engine still idling. Big garbageman God, sitting behind the wheel of his truckful of crap, casually looking up toward the house.

What's his deal? I thought. I opened the window and let him have it. "Hey. What's your problem? Get lost. It's none of your business if I decide to live with my trash for another week. Maybe I'll keep it two weeks. What's it to you, anyway? Scram!"

And he did. Slowly he pulled away.

The next week definitely had an odor about it. It was weird how the smell followed me around. I don't think other people could tell, but I just couldn't get away from it. It clung to me like seaweed; like a twenty-pound sack of dead mackerel draped around my neck.

When next Thursday came I was happy to traipse my two weeks' of stinking, stockpiled trash to the end of the driveway. It took four trips. As I arrived with the last ripe package, God pulled up in his shiny truck.

"Mornin'," he chirped like a bird who'd just excavated a fat juicy worm. He inhaled and caught a lungful of my toxic waste.

"Ooowee. Bet you'll be glad to be rid of this."

I was. It had been stinking up the whole house, the whole neighborhood.

"Sorry about last Thursday," I said sheepishly. "I didn't

mean to yell at you. Well, at least I know now that you don't come up to the house to get the trash."

"No sirree. You gotta bring it to the curb—and leave it there. Until you decide that it's trash and bring it on down, I can't touch it. I'd like to. But, we got rules you know." We both nodded.

"Well, if that's everything, I better get back at it. The world's not gettin' any cleaner just lookin' at it." I heard a "Heh, heh, heh" as he climbed back into the cab, and he was gone. So was my trash, and that smell that had been hounding me for two weeks.

The next week I was on top of things. Gathered up all the junk the night before and even hauled it out late Wednesday evening. It felt good. I woke up, took the dog for a walk, grabbed the newspaper from the mailbox, and started heading back up to the house.

As I was passing the garbage something caught my eye. It was a Tupperware container of something I had enjoyed several days ago. *I wonder if that's still good?* I thought. *It doesn't look that bad. I bet I could have that for one—more—meal.* I looked around to see if anybody was watching, then I grabbed my little Tupperware container of lust and started walking double-time back up to the house.

I hadn't gone more than three paces when I heard it—

the downshifting of God's ten-ton truck. Man! His timing was incredible. How could he sneak up on me with that 400-horsepower Jimmy?

"Hey, I can take that for you!" he yelled as he jumped from the truck before it had even stopped rolling. "That looks like it's gone bad. It'll just smell up your refrigerator."

I knew he was right but I wanted it. That lust had tasted so good when I had stirred it up a few days ago. I wanted it for just one more meal. What could it hurt? I'd throw it out next week.

"No, that's OK, God. This is still good," I said in a phony singsong voice that didn't sound convincing even to me. "It's—it's only two days old—doesn't smell at all."

"You sure?"

"Yeah. No problem. See you next week." He walked with me back up to the garage. Him with the empty cans and me with my leftovers. Neither of us said a word.

That night I pulled that Tupperware container out of the fridge. One minute in the microwave and that little hot dish was steaming. The first bite was good but by the sixth or seventh I couldn't taste the sweet anymore, only the sour. My stomach delivered the message that my mind already knew. I should have left it at the curb. Once I carry it out, I should let him bury it.

I never slept that night. In fact, about three that morning I got out the Yellow Pages, dialed up my trashman, and roused him out of bed.

He answered on the first ring. Said he'd be right over. When I opened the door he was already there, waiting at the end of the driveway, standing beside his truck. He met me halfway to the curb. I handed him the scattered remains in the Tupperware dish. He took it with both hands like I'd just given him a treasure. Then he did something no garbageman had ever done for me before. He wrapped his arms around me in a hug that almost seemed to squeeze the impure past from my bones. I felt like I'd been washed and waxed from the inside out. Free. Clean. Forgiven.

As he turned to leave, my eye caught the Tupperware dish in his hands. To my surprise, it was full again. More than full. The top was just barely balancing on the heaping mound of stench that had been mine. I cringed as I saw it seeping out and running onto his palms. I saw him wince as my garbage pierced the purity of his hands . . . but he never said a word.

As he drove away I realized that I was clean, but only at his expense.

Is it possible that he could have squeezed the depths of

past trash right out of me with that hug? Have I been missing something when I just bring my cans of trash to the curb? Maybe I need to deliver *myself* to the curb and let him remove everything that's unclean from me every time I see him; let him go through the cupboards and drawers of my soul and leave me brand-new.

My garbageman and I have a whole new relationship now. We're close. We have a great understanding. I generate junk in amazing amounts and he scours me down till I shine like the sun. I create trash and he removes it. It seems unfair for him but he never complains. And for me, hey, it's the deal of a lifetime.

To this day I've never received a bill from God's Garbage Removal. A couple of times I've caught him at the curb and offered him money. He always declines, says that knowing I'm clean again is all the payment he wants. Have you ever heard something so unbelievable? But I'm telling you, I swear, it's the God's honest truth!

The Hitchhiker

It was Christmas morning. I stood on the shoulder
of Interstate 80 somewhere in the middle of Wyoming,
blowing on my hands trying to keep them pliable. I had my
thumb out in a pose I'd seen in countless movies, but one
I'd never struck myself.

I think it was the angel perched on the tip of our Christmas
tree that gave me the idea. It wasn't a vision or anything like
that, just a harebrained scheme to go in search of Mecca, a
Norman Rockwellian utopia. Heaven. That was my plan.
Plain and simple; thumb my way to heaven. So I packed a
lunch, grabbed my boots, and headed for the highway.

I had used a green magic marker to scratch my destination of choice on an old piece of cardboard.

Heaven.

That's all it said.

I'd been sitting there for about an hour. Three uneventful rides had taken me this far. Still, no heaven in sight. Sixty-eight cars had gone by since the last ride had dumped me here. He'd only taken me a few miles, just far enough to get me out into the sticks. Then he pulled over, reached across my lap, threw open my door, and basically told me where to go, which, incidentally, wasn't heaven. As he kicked me out onto the shoulder I heard his hacking laugh over the screech of tires, a nice little punctuation on his prank. *That's OK,* I thought. *I didn't figure him for the kind of guy with a nose for heaven anyway.*

I'm not sure I really know what heaven is. Would I recognize it if I saw it? Will there be a sign when I enter that says,

Heaven

Population 4,317,462?

When I was a kid I thought Christmas morning was about as close to heaven as you could get. All the presents and food, and everybody happy. Seemed all right to me.

I don't know, maybe it's out there, maybe it isn't. But hey, it's Christmas Day; who knows, maybe I'll get lucky.

Just then a beat-up pickup truck pulled over onto the shoulder. The door had a big crease in the side, the obvious victim of a head-butt from a misguided fender. This certainly didn't have the appearance of a ticket to heaven, but I grabbed my backpack, ran up to the truck, and pried open the passenger door.

"Ho, ho, ho," came at me with a tired, fairy-tale delivery. The driver, a fiftyish man of considerable girth, smiled at me displaying a black hole where a bicuspid and an incisor belonged. He was dressed in red velvet from head to toe. The fake white beard hung from his neck by a rubber strap. It reminded me of a bib my nephew used to wear, complete with ketchup stains.

I reached out my hand to him and said, "Merry Christmas, Santa."

"I'm not going to heaven, but I can take you as far as the North Pole," he chuckled. Then he did that clicking sound with his tongue, cracked an imaginary whip, and said, "Come on, Rudolf, let's go." His right foot went all the way to the floor and his 2.3-liter team of reindeer dug their hooves into the asphalt. After a spit, a sputter, and a backfire, we were off.

We rode in silence for a couple of minutes. Then Santa looked at me, sizing me up. "Heaven, huh?"

"Yup."

"I suppose you don't believe in me then. You'd be more of a Jesus fan than Santa."

"I'm just trying to get to heaven. If you can get me there, hey, I'll believe in you." I meant it. I was an ends-justifies-the-means kind of guy. I figured whoever knows how to get there must be the man.

Another minute of silence.

"A kid asked me once if I could make sure his dog was in heaven."

"What'd you say?"

"I said, 'Sonny, he's already there.'" A jagged grin jiggled his jowls. He took off his hat and placed it on the dashboard. The move uncovered a scalp that was uncovering itself. Even the Grecian formula combover couldn't hide the fact.

Santa looked at me. "You gotta die first, you know."

"Excuse me?"

"Heaven. You gotta die first. Can't go there till you die. Otherwise what would be the point of earth? Shoot, this would be heaven . . . and it ain't. Pretty dang sure 'bout that."

We pulled into Cheyenne, filled up, grabbed a Coke, and turned north on 25 toward Casper. On the way out of town we hit a red light right beside a Holiday Inn motel. In place of the normal "No Vacancy" sign were the words "No Room in the Inn."

"Everyone's a comedian," I half whispered under my breath. The light turned green . . . and we sat there. I looked over at Santa to see if he had dozed off, but instead I saw him staring toward the Holiday Inn sign. I looked over there and saw what had caught his eye. Sitting under the sign was another hitchhiker. He was holding a hand-made cardboard sign almost identical to mine, except it read,

Earth.

"I'll be diggety dogged," said Santa. "This I don't wanna miss." He pulled over, I slid over, and Mr. Earth hopped in.

"Ho, ho, ho!" Déjà vu all over again.

"Hi, guys. Thanks for the lift," said Mr. Earth.

"Mr. Earth, meet Mr. Heaven . . . I'm Mr. Claus." Three crazies in the front seat of a rusted-out '88 Dodge Dakota. Once more, fiction bowed to the superseding strangeness of truth. Santa put his shoe leather to the rear end of Donner and Blitzen and we were off. Nobody said anything for a while. Finally I ventured, "Merry Christmas."

Mr. Earth looked at me, then at my sign. "Heaven, huh?"

"Yup."

"You'll like it there. It's nice."

Oh boy, I thought, *I'm sitting next to a wacko. He thinks he's been to heaven.*

"Don't tell me; you're a philosophy major, right?" offered Santa.

"More or less."

"I knew it."

Then, out of nowhere, "Hey, it's my birthday today," offered Mr. Earth.

"No kidding?" Santa looked at me, and without so much as a glimmer of reservation, he busted out into song with a voice that I imagined would be how Elvis would sound now, were he still alive.

> Happy birthday to you (Honk)
> Happy birthday to you (Honk)
> Happy birthday . . . Mr. Earth
> Happy birthday to you.

I clapped, Santa honked some more, and Mr. Earth tipped his head in thanks.

"So, how old did you say you were?" I asked.

"Hmm, that's a hard question." Mr. Earth appeared to be in a bit of a fog. "I feel ancient, but today, back there at the inn, I felt newborn. Strange, huh?"

"Christmas will do that to ya," said Santa. "It's the cure for what ails you. Makes you feel like a kid again."

Our newest passenger snapped out of his daze, looked at me like he was psychoanalyzing me, and asked, "So, what don't you like about earth? Why are you trying to leave it?"

"Oh, I like it," I said, "but something's missing. I always feel like there must be something else, something more, something beyond . . ." I trailed off into thought.

Mr. Earth smiled at me knowingly and said, "You *are* going to like heaven."

Santa looked at Mr. Earth for a full ten seconds without looking back at the road. You could tell he had his mental yardstick out and was measuring the depth of the topsoil of Mr. Terra Firma. He finally looked back at the road and stated very matter-of-factly, "You're an alien, ain't ya?"

"Well, I'm not from around here, if that's what you mean." Mr. Earth looked straight ahead, downplaying the fact that he'd just swerved to miss a head-on question.

This guy was starting to give me the creeps. I decided to put him on the spot, take away his turn lane so his answer would have to stay between the lines. "All right, so who are you and what do you . . . ?"

Just then Santa put the sleigh into a four-hoof skid. Mr. Earth and I grabbed for the dash, hoping to keep from sailing through the windshield. As the Dakota rocked to a stop I noticed why Santa had yanked so hard on the reins. There in front of us, all the way across the road, was a herd of sheep. A couple hundred or more.

"What the—" Santa rolled out of the truck, tripping on his belt, which had burst and was now wrapped around his ankles. He looked like he was going to blow up, but then he just started laughing. Two guys who were evidently herding the sheep across the road came running up to check on him.

"You OK?" they asked.

"Yeah. Wasn't exactly expecting to run across a herd of sheep in the middle of Highway 25 though."

"Sorry. Something gave them a scare up there on the hill and they took off runnin'. I'm, I'm really sorry. Here, we'll uh, move 'em, make a path for you to drive through, and you can be on your way." For the first time it seemed the shepherd noticed the red velvet getup. Then he quipped, "Don't want a bunch of angry kids blaming us for a ruined Christmas, now do we?"

Ah, a shepherd with a sense of humor.

As we made our way through the herd, Mr. Earth rolled down his window and appeared to be evaluating each sheep as we passed. When we got to the end, he leaned out toward one of the shepherds and said, "Better check on Evelyn. She's got a burr in her right front hoof."

Yikes! All I could think was, *I hope Mr. Earth's not packin' heat.*

I was about to gently revisit my questions for him when Mr. Earth started singing under his breath. The song was "Santa Claus is Coming to Town," and he was building up steam with each phrase.

Santa, in his best fat Elvis, started crooning along with what was obviously his favorite song.

I decided to abandon my line of questions and my cynicism and join them.

We had just finished the verse about the "list" and who's "naughty and nice" when Mr. Earth interrupted the chorus of three tenors with another one of his obscure statements. "You know, Santa, you and I are a lot alike. We both have a list—we both know who's naughty and nice. Hey, what do you give the naughty ones?"

Santa gave him that what-a-stupid-question look. "Nothin'," he answered. "You kiddin'?'"

"Ah, that's where you and I are different. Actually that's why I'm here . . . for the naughty ones, I guess."

Santa, thinking: "Hey, between you and me we got the whole world covered then, right?"

Mr. Earth, smiling: "To be honest, I think I've got it covered just on my side of things. I mean nobody's perfect, so in a sense, everybody's—naughty."

I was going to jump in there, but I thought I'd let those two hammer it out.

"So, um, what you gonna do for 'em, the naughty ones?"

Mr. Earth seemed to think about that for a while. He cocked his head a bit and said, "I'm going to give them an eraser; a gift that will give them a clean piece of paper again. A fresh start."

I couldn't resist jumping in. "You mean, like a denaughtyizer?"

"Yeah. A denaughtyizer. I like that."

"So," chimed in Santa, "where's the naughty gonna go? A landfill or something?"

"No. I'm . . . I'm going to carry it."

I half laughed. "It's a big world and there's no shortage of evil. Do you realize the weight of the load you're talking about?"

"Yeah."

I looked in his eyes, and for the first time I realized they weren't the eyes of a wacko. They were clear. I could see all the way to the bottom, sheer honesty.

"You're, you're aware a load like that could kill you, right?" I asked.

He looked out the side window, and almost to himself he said, "Yeah."

Do you ever have those moments where truth knifes through the fog and slashes away at what you thought was real? In that instant, my view of reality was rerouted. The old map of my life was made up of circular randomness, a robotic progression toward nothing. But in his eyes, I saw coordinates that were clear, purposeful, and true. I know this sounds crazy, but suddenly I knew who I was, where I was going, and who could show me the way there.

I looked at Mr. Earth and said, "You're the eraser, aren't you."

"Yeah."

There I sat between a Santa who serviced the good, the nice, the flawless; and a nouveau Santa incarnate of sorts whose clientele was the bad eggs of the world. I knew from which dozen I had hatched, and I knew which Santa carried the sack with the gift I needed.

Still looking out the window, far away, Mr. Earth said, "I'm going to hitchhike the face of the earth till everyone who's looking for something more has a chance to find it. Till everyone with a smudged list is offered the eraser. Till everyone with a handmade cardboard sign gets directions."

I looked at Mr. Earth and said, "You know, I could use an eraser myself—and I certainly could use some directions."

He smiled, then looked over at Santa. "Mr. Claus, you with us?"

Even with Santa's lopsided grin I could tell he was in. "You just tell old St. Nick where to go and my team will take you there."

Just then I got an idea. "Pull over for a second, will you, Santa? There's something I gotta do." As we coasted to a stop, I climbed over Mr. Earth and walked around the backside of the truck. I took my "Heaven" sign and wedged it into the frame around the license plate.

"There. That should help." I hopped in and Santa nudged the team back up to speed.

It was Christmas Day in the middle of Wyoming. The best present I ever got was riding next to me in the front seat of a truck. Life is a strange ride.

We were halfway through "Jingle Bell Rock" when three guys pulled up beside us in a Camel cigarette delivery truck. The guy on the passenger side rolled down his window and motioned for Santa to do the same. He leaned out and yelled, "Hey, St. Nick, I got a present for you and your buddies." He threw three Cracker Jack boxes through our window and then dropped back in line right behind us.

"Wise guys," said Santa as he handed out the treats. We opened our boxes complete with their toy surprises. Santa got a fake gold ring in his box, I got a plastic action figure of Frankenstein, and Mr. Earth got a tattoo of Papa Smurf.

Gold, Frankenstein, and Smurf. Go figure.

"Wow. Nobody ever gave me a gift on Christmas before," said Santa. Mr. Earth looked at him and grinned till his dimples showed. I turned to look through the back window and give a wave of thanks to our philanthropic Camel couriers.

I wasn't prepared for what came next. My eyes were met by a billion-watt barrage of light. Headlights snaking around curves and over hills as far as I could see. It was like the whole world had been strung with chasing Christmas tree lights. There must have been a convoy of a million cars and trucks in our wake, each one paying tribute to the man who knew the way.

We finished singing "Jingle Bell Rock" as we headed toward the sunset. The road sign said we were still in Wyoming, but I swore I could see heaven from there.

I learned something today. Heaven's not as far away as it seems. It's just a matter of putting your thumb out, hitching a ride, and saying, "Follow that rusted-out '88 Dodge Dakota. The one with the handmade cardboard sign for a license plate."

Bum Insurance

They called him Mr. Insurance. He peddled his policies from the front of a rickety old shopping cart. The sidewalks and alleys of downtown Chicago were his region—from the lakefront, over to State Street, and on down to the river. He punched in around noon and sold till the streets emptied.

Stubby fingers poked through unintentionally holey gloves. His soiled Bulls stocking cap hadn't left his head in three months. He wore a ruptured Air Jordan on his left foot and some indiscernible brand of hiking boot on his right. Neither had come with a box or receipt.

"There's hope for now if you got hope for later," he said

as he skittered along the gutter. It was hard to tell if he was driving the cart or if the cart was driving him.

". . . hope for now if you got hope for later." Only the occasional passerby would acknowledge his existence.

I met him on a Friday night. My partner and I were patrolling along Michigan Avenue, zigzagging our blue-and-white down every alley on our beat. It was 10:30 and I was getting sleepy, that tiredness that comes five hours into a sedentary shift.

"You want some coffee?" I asked midyawn. "I'm gonna need a little mojo buzz if I'm gonna make it to midnight."

"Yeah, I guess I could use a hit myself," said Kelly. Kelly was my partner—pretty new to the force. Still a bit green, but good, solid cop potential. I liked him.

I'd been cruising the streets of Chi-town for twenty-two years. Pretty much seen it all. Muggings, murders, accidents. Made a million arrests—everything from jaywalking to drug dealing. Not a cushy job, but I liked it—it fit me.

I jumped out of our car and headed into a little corner coffee shop. An orange neon sign over the door flashed, "Funky Java." I'd been coming here for bean for three or four years now. It was one of those retro-looking joints that made me feel at home—garage sale tables and chairs in all the colors of the tie-dyed '60s, complete with lava lamps and macramé wall hangings. They played old Crosby Stills and Nash. Doors, Hendrix, and Joplin. I could hear the nostalgic rhythm in the aroma before I smelled it.

"Hey, Benny. How's the street looking tonight?"

Roxanne was one of the few people on the face of the earth that could get away with calling me Benny. She naturally disarmed people. Her smile always cut about a half-hour off my eight-hour shift. In fact, if I were to be totally honest, I didn't really come here for the coffee as much as I did for Roxanne. I got more buzz from her smile than her coffee.

"Hi, Rox. So far, so good. Everybody's acting like adults for a change. Must be drinking your brew." She smiled and turned to get what I always got without me having to say a word.

"There's hope for now if you got hope for later."

I turned to see who was talking at me. He was only about five-four, but stood tall, maximizing every last inch of his hunched frame. He stood next to his shopping cart, holding several sheets of paper out to me.

"I'm sorry," said Roxanne, "haven't you two met? Benny, this is my friend Mr. Insurance. Mr. Insurance, this is Mr. Gentle Gun-toting Ben." She winked at me.

"Pleased to meet you, Mr. Ben. Do you got life insurance?"

"Yeah, I've got a policy—somewhere. Not gonna make anybody rich, but they'll be able to put me in a hole plus a few grand or so for my sister in Atlanta. That's about it."

"No, I mean *life* insurance, Mr. Ben. Not money insurance, or casket insurance. 'At don't do you no good. You still dead." He raised his eyebrows and gave me that "are you trackin' with me" look. I turned to Roxanne for some feedback, but she just shrugged her shoulders, which I took to mean, "Hey, figure him out for yourself."

I've been dealing with homeless people for years. Some of them are crazies, but for the most part I've come to see them as people who got a bad break, took a fall, and just couldn't seem to climb back into the world. I was trying to figure out which category Mr. Insurance fit into. I took the papers from his hand, figuring it might lend a clue as to the state of his mental whereabouts.

The top of the paper simply read, "Life Insurance for Bums." It was almost like a contract, very neatly organized into articles, paragraphs, points, and subpoints. Very legal-looking, except for the fact that it was all handwritten—all six pages of it. And it appeared that he had dozens of these contracts in his shopping cart. It had to represent hundreds of hours of dragging a pen across paper. Staggering. Had he never heard of Kinko's?

It took me a while to find the hook, the epicenter of his scam. I found it on the bottom of page two. There was no section in this policy pertaining to beneficiaries because—and get this—according to the contract, the holder of this policy would not die. In fact, this policy claimed to give the bearer eternal life.

Well, at least now I knew in which category to put Mr. Insurance. Had to be the crazy bin. What could be more illogical than a decaying hobo marketing the fountain of youth? I mean, I've seen people break the laws of the Sixth Precinct before, but physical laws, like death? I don't think so. Dying always came with a chiseled-in-stone certainty.

I decided to play along, let him take me for a whole buck or two. "So, how much for the policy?" I asked, reaching for my wallet.

"Free. It's free. Didn't you read page four? Says right there." He pointed out the section. Sure enough, free. Not a red cent. Eternal life for nothin'. Just sign your name and forever was yours for the taking.

"Seems, uh, too good to be true, Mr. Insurance."

"It is . . . but that don't make it not true. True doesn't always make as much sense as you think it should." He thought for a second, then finished with, "True is or isn't—it's not ours to decide."

I nodded. I had to admit there was less idiot in this savant than I had originally thought.

He looked at me like he was still waiting for a decision. In his mind he'd just offered me his prize produce for free and couldn't imagine why I wouldn't want to take a bite.

"What's wrong, Mr. Ben? Can't afford free?" He saw me looking at the heading on page one, the "Life Insurance for Bums" title.

"Ah," he said. "You're still looking in the Fun House mirror." He paused, glancing at the ceiling, then went on, "The way I see it, the whole world's made up of two groups, bums and potential bums. Mr. Ben, I'm afraid you just haven't realized your potential yet." He laughed a hacking laugh, then, more thoughtfully, he finished with, "It's hard. Nobody wants to look at a bum . . . especially when he's looking back at you in the mirror. But it's OK. Tell you what, bein' the generous insurance agent that I am, I'm going to sign a policy right now and put your name on it. It'll be waitin' here. You come back to me when you've seen the reflection of you that is, not the one that might be."

He turned and started walking toward a corner table. "Besides," he continued without turning around, "this policy won't work till you know you ain't nothin' but a bum."

As he sat down at the table he exhaled his final thought. "The policy is for bums."

I leaned an elbow on the counter and Roxanne proceeded to tell me about this little philanthropist of whole-life. It turns out he'd been around for only a month or two and already nearly 80 percent of the downtown homeless carried his paperwork on them. A sort of street brand of antisocial security.

He also carried a rubber stamper, the kind you'd push into a pad of ink and then stamp on a piece of paper. His stamp simply said, "Insured for Life." After a person signed a policy, he would stamp the back of their hand with red ink. "There. You're covered," he would say. The homeless had come to see him almost like a savior, issuing hope stamps to the hopeless.

Kelly, who had tired of waiting for me in the car, joined me at the counter. He took his coffee and a newspaper and headed for a back corner table. Roxanne gave me a refill and a double shot of her caffeinated grin, and I went to join Kelly.

We were finishing our drinks when a guy walked through the door carrying a revolverful of trouble. He had a stocking cap pulled over his face. He charged straight up to Roxanne, grabbed her by the hair, put the gun to her head and started yelling, "Nobody move or she dies!" The place went silent except for Crosby Stills and Nash coming from the stereo.

> *Our house, is a very, very, very fine house.*
> *With two cats in the . . .*

A shot rang out and the CD player breathed its last.

"I hate cats." He slowly looked around the room as if analyzing each person. "Anybody here own a cat?" Not a sound. "Good. You're smart people. Stay that way for a few minutes and I might let you live."

He directed Roxanne to empty the register and put the money in a bag. Kelly and I were in a dark enough corner that he couldn't see our uniforms. We both had our hands on our guns. Both waiting for the right moment, both not wanting to put Roxanne in any danger.

I don't know how he got up there without being noticed, but all of a sudden we heard, "There's hope for now if you got hope for later."

The gunman wheeled to square up with the voice. I thought for sure Mr. Insurance was about to find out the cash value of his policy. "Sit down and shut up, ya stupid bum."

My grip tightened on my gun.

I've never seen a more complete lack of fear in my life. I've been in hundreds of situations like this and I'm always afraid. My heart always pounds a hole in my chest. Mr. Insurance looked like he could have played a game of Pickup Sticks, he was so calm.

Mr. Insurance broke in again, "There's hope for now if you got hope for later."

"What are you talkin' about?"

Mr. Insurance cocked his head a bit and took a half step toward the gunman. "I know what you want, and it ain't money. It's what you think you can *buy* with money. You want hope, but hope ain't for sale."

The robber stared at him for a while and then chuckled, and then started laughing harder and harder till he was almost convulsing. Kelly thought about making his move but I put a hand on his arm to stop him. Our thief abruptly cut off his laughter, turned and put his gun up the nostril of Mr. Insurance. He leaned into his words with a low, steely delivery. "What would a loser like you know about hope? There is no hope for scum like us. We're born trash and we'll die trash. That's it. End of story." He backed off.

I could see sweat on Roxanne's forehead. Her heart had to be doing a hundred fifty or so. Mr. Insurance, still in a dead calm groove stated, "The money you just took? You don't need it. You can't buy what you want with it . . . cuz what you want is free."

"And what exactly is it that I want, Mr. piece-of-garbage know-it-all?"

Mr. Insurance slowly reached into his shopping cart and pulled out a policy. "This." he said, as he handed it to the thief. The stocking-capped gunman held it with the hand he had wrapped around Roxanne's neck. He put his cheek up to hers as he scanned the contents. Page two caught his attention.

"Eternal freakin' life. Ha, ha!" He let out a yelp of glee and started dragging Roxanne from table to table, asking customers, "Do you got yours yet? Hey cart man, get over here, this lady ain't got no ticket to heaven. Hurry up!" Directed by a loaded pistol, Mr. Insurance put some papers in front of her and she signed. The thief looked at Mr. Insurance and said, "That's it? That's all there is to it?"

Mr. Insurance pulled his rubber stamper from the cart and said, "Well, I usually finish by stamping their hands with this."

"Well, go ahead then." His sarcasm marched on. "I don't want to be responsible for messing up her future."

Mr. Insurance pressed the stamper into the red ink pad

and then branded the backs of both her hands. "There. You're covered," he said as he looked into her eyes.

The thief appeared to be enjoying this little game. He approached another table, at this one a businessman with a briefcase and a *Wall Street Journal*. The thief walked up to him, Roxanne still in tow, and asked in his best salesman-like voice, "Excuse me, sir, have you gotten your policy for eternal life yet? This might be something you should consider." The businessman nodded and the thief motioned for Mr. Insurance to bring a policy. The contract was set down on the table and turned to page six. Mr. Insurance started to hand the pen to the businessman, but then paused and looked at the thief in a pleading way and said, "Please, don't do this."

The gunman ground the barrel deeper into Roxanne's temple and cinched his arm around her neck. I could see her wince under the pressure. The thief's voice went cold again. Looking hard into Mr. Insurance's eyes, he said, "Do it."

Mr. Insurance reluctantly handed the pen to the businessman, who seemed unnerved by this dialogue. As he put his hand down to the paper to sign, the thief arced the gun toward the forehead of the businessman, stopping between his eyes. I looked away just before he pulled the trigger. The sound echoed for a second, followed by a few screams that quickly settled into restrained sobs. The gun was instantly back to Roxanne's head. I felt helpless, useless.

The thief was still staring at the lifeless businessman. I noticed something strange. The gunman had tears in his eyes and his hand was shaking. He quickly tried to wipe the betraying tears away with the barrel of his gun, but there seemed to be plenty more where those came from. He tried to regroup, mustering up a snarly dose of rehearsed cynicism. Still in a shaky voice he said, "What a shame. He was just seconds away from living forever." He sighed and looked at Mr. Insurance through eyes flooded with years of pain and hurt. Then he said in a choking whisper, "You never really know how much time you got left, do ya?"

Then, with his left arm still around Roxanne's neck, he slowly moved the pistol from her temple to his own. He pulled the hammer back with his thumb, the tremble of his hand now exaggerated. He squeezed his eyes shut as hard as he could, searching for the courage to pull the plug on his own life.

Mr. Insurance took a step toward the murderer. He put his hand up as if to say, Wait. Without looking away he reached in his cart and pulled out a contract. He held it out to the killer and offered, "There's still hope for now . . ." He paused, then continued, "If—if you got hope for later." The whole room held its breath. For fifteen seconds all we heard was the one-note prayer of the refrigerator compressor.

Mr. Insurance continued, "You were a bum before you walked in here tonight. You were a bum before you stole from Roxanne. You were a bum before you murdered that man." Mr. Insurance looked at the man on the floor, then back up at the hooded face. "You're still just a bum, no more, no less." He took a long, slow breath. "And this contract . . . it can still cover you."

The killer couldn't hold on anymore. The mask was crumbling. His arm still collared Roxanne's neck, but the gun was now hanging at his side. His head hung low as he said, "How?" He looked at Mr. Insurance pleadingly. "How can a no-good piece of trash like me still qualify for something so unbelievable?"

"The owner of this company paid a great price to make this policy available—to you. Look." Mr. Insurance opened the policy to page six and showed him the place for his signature. Underneath the line designated for the policyholder it said "James Lloyd Stanley." The killer lowered his head, squinting, wondering if he was seeing things. He touched the barrel of his revolver to his name on the contract.

Mr. Insurance took the chin of the killer in his hand and

lifted it so he would look into his eyes. "You can't be bad enough that this contract won't cover you. Stop running, turn around. Take off your mask. The owner wants to cover you."

James, the murderer, released Roxanne for the first time in a half-hour. She sank to the floor, exhausted. He pulled the cap off his head as Mr. Insurance slid the gun from his hand.

"You knew I was going to shoot that guy. You knew my name. Who are you?"

"I'm your—insurance agent." Mr. Insurance gently set the gun on the counter. James signed his name to the contract of hope. Above the line requiring the agent's signature, in sweeping penmanship, Mr. Insurance signed "Heysoose." James smiled at Heysoose . . . the first time he'd used those muscles in years.

It was the very last thing he ever did as a free man. Kelly locked the cuffs on his wrists and started walking him toward the door. Mr. Insurance called out to him and Kelly pulled James to a stop and turned. Heysoose took James tenderly by the hands, reached out with his rubber stamper, and sealed the contract with his red ink.

"There. You're covered."

James looked at the "Insured for Life" lettering on his hands. He noticed that Heysoose, too, had red stains on the backs of his hands, but they were no longer legible. They almost looked like scars from an ancient wound. Mr. Insurance wiped a tear from James's cheek and reassured him, "You're covered."

Kelly took James in another car while I stayed to take care of things at the scene. I didn't get out of there till 2:30 in the morning. I was headed for home, tired and emotionally spent, when I happened to get a glimpse of myself in the rearview mirror. This time the mirror stared back at me. I saw the reflection that is, not the one that might be. I saw malnourished eyes, deep-set with hunger. I saw rags. I saw hopelessness.

I saw a cop wearing a Bulls cap.

I saw a bum.

I made an illegal U-turn right in front of the Crate and Barrel store on Michigan Avenue. I pointed my car back toward Roxanne's with the intention of finding Heysoose and that six-page mortality waiver. I went back to get covered.

On Saturday the *Tribune* reported a murder at Funky Java, but that's not the whole story. Today there's an altruistic insurance agent on the corner of Grand and St. Clair cavalierly dispensing life to the dying, with the words "There's hope for now if you got hope for later."

To Tell The Truth

You remember the show. Gary Moore, Orson Bean, Kitty Carlisle, Peggy Cass, and Tom Poston. That '60's-ish stark set, slicked hair, and contestants that came in threes. Remember Saturday nights, watching it on a black-and-white tube TV with the rabbit ears pointing northeast and southwest?

Which two were the impostors and which one the genuine article? Was it fake-fraud-genuine, fake-genuine-fraud, or genuine-fake-fraud? Truth and lies couched in shades of gray, the innocent suspense of a bygone era.

As part of my job bringing old shows back into syndication, I had been assigned to preview the *To Tell the Truth* library and make recommendations to the various cable bidders. In digging through the files of old shows in the network archives, I came across an episode that had never run. It had been pulled from circulation. There was a note attached to it that simply said, "Do not air!" I popped it in to see what had warranted this particular show getting the hook. It didn't take long for the answer to unfold. Here's what I found . . .

The Colgate jingle ended and the ruse began—distinguishing the real deal from the clones.

They walked out onto the stage in silhouette, backlit to enhance the mystery. The first contestant was wearing sandals and some kind of animal skin, wrapped and tied with a length of rope.

"*My* name is Jesus Christ."

Number Two was sporting the flowing-white-robe look, complete with the long wavy hair parted down the middle. His feet were also planted firmly in a sandal of the times . . . Birkenstocks.

"My *name* is Jesus Christ."

Number Three was definitely the odd man out. A blue oxford shirt, Levi's, and hiking boots. He looked comfortable but not very Christlike.

"My name is *Jesus Christ*."

By way of introduction, Gary was reading what amounted to a résumé for the Holy One.

"The son of a carpenter, purportedly born of a virgin, this man claims to be the Son of God. He has performed many amazing feats, including turning water into wine and feeding thousands with only a few fish and bread. He has healed the lame, given sight to the blind, and some say he has even raised the dead. He predicts his future will hold his death, his resurrection, and a kingdom that will never end. Please welcome, Jesus Christ."

The walk-on music kicked in, the lights came up, and the lopsided trinity took their seats.

Orson started the questioning. "OK, let's say, just for the sake of argument, that I was a murderer, and I happened upon you in a dark alley, decided to rob and kill you. What would be your response to me in that situation—Jesus Number One?"

Wow. That was a tough one. Jesus Number One's mind was red-lining. Nothing like getting out of the gates in a dead sprint. "Well . . ." He drew out his words, hoping the stagecoach of wisdom would arrive on time. "I'm opposed to violence . . . so I guess I would have to . . . to . . . (whinny, whinny) turn the other cheek!" Whew!

The Pony Express dumped that package of truth in his

mouth with only seconds to spare. The thin ice hardened under the sandals of Jesus Number One and Orson proceeded on down the line. "Jesus Number Two, same question."

This guy was primed and ready to go. His stagecoach had arrived so long ago that the horses had already been fed and watered. "First off," he said with chin-in-the-air confidence, "I would smite you with leprosy, then in your incapacitated state I would explain to you how murder is sin and goes against my plan for the world, not to mention the sixth commandment. Then, in my divine wisdom, I would restore you to health and send you on your way, a new, reborn man."

This time the applause needed no prompting. It was spontaneous. Early results from the exit polls were showing that the crowd liked a jujitsu Jesus, one of action, one who didn't hesitate to use his power.

Orson continued, "And Jesus Number Three, how would you respond to my attempting to murder you?"

The blue-oxford Jesus had no trouble coming up with his response either. "I'd run."

The panel and the crowd seemed to pause, anticipating a measure of clarification. When they realized there was none forthcoming, a few chuckles broke through the

silence. There was a degree of humor in this—an all-powerful creator, God incarnate, scrambling over garbage cans
to escape one of his own bad-seed creations. Not a very
Yahwehish picture.

Gary pulled in the reins and handed them over to Kitty.
"Your question, Miss Carlisle."

She looked up and down the trio of Jesuses (or is it Jesi?),
as if hoping to discover hidden x-ray vision leaking from an
eye. Having failed to discern a flaw of supernatural conse-
quence, she resorted to the due diligence of questioning.

"Jesus Number Two. If you are, as you claim, God incarnate, why do you say you must die?"

Again, Number Two, the Quick Draw McGraw of the
threesome, fired away, "I have raised others from the dead.
But the ultimate display, the proof, if you will, of my
superhuman deity will be displayed when I, unaided by
human hands, drag myself back from the bowels of death,
and return, gloriously, to my rightful place as King of kings
and Lord of lords."

The always-looking-for-a-sign crowd loved this answer.
After all, each of them thought, *if I were God, wouldn't I use
every opportunity to prove my divinity, to flex my mystical mus-
cle, to swing my righteous fists of fire? Darn right, I would. I'd be
a regular indestructible Jackie-Chan Jesus. Jean-Claude Van Christ.*

The crowd was buying in. Big time. Old Mo was swinging in the direction of the white-robed Jesus. Yeah, signs and wonders—can't get enough of 'em.

Kitty continued, "Jesus Number One. Let's say you die . . . crucified, whatever. Then something gets messed up and you can't quite pull off the resurrection part. Sunday comes, and you don't. Are you still God? Would that rule out your claims of deity?"

The three hundred bucks that Jesus Number One was getting paid to perform this charade suddenly seemed grossly inadequate. He was actually starting to get peeved by the fact that they were questioning his fabricated superhero status. It's one thing to fake it, but quite another to be called on it.

He proceeded, "Isn't it enough to know that I lived a life of perfection?" He spit the words out with a pinch of righteous indignation. "Isn't it enough to know that I taught love and compassion? That I healed the sick, lifted up the downtrodden, cared for the unloved?"

The cadence quickened.

"If I die and am never raised, will that negate the love I shared, the lives I touched? No! A life lived well is a thing of beauty. A treasure of great value."

Now, with an avalanche of passion.

"In two thousand years, if I am only seen as a great teacher, an example of humanity at its best, then that will be enough for me. I will have left my mark on the world. For I will have been God for a season!"

What a recovery. It was like watching a Rocky movie. He was down for the count and now, miraculously, was flailing away like a champ.

The crowd loved his spunk. This was an underdog Jesus. A moldable Jesus. One who wasn't so black-and-white. One who was willing to admit his own limitations, his own . . . mortality.

Finally. A God who was more human.

A few of the tender-hearted in the crowd couldn't keep the sobs to themselves. The poignancy potion had been dispensed.

Kitty, taking a cue from the producer to keep things moving, started asking Jesus Number Three, "If time were relative, and . . ."

"I'm sorry, Kitty, but if I may, please, respond to the last few questions," said Jesus Number Three, stepping on her line. Kitty nodded. He took off his glasses and rubbed his eyes for a moment. Was it possible that this Jesus could pull a rabbit out of his hat as well? Could he recover from his lame "I'd run" line?

He began, "Life . . . is important to me. But love, even more so." He paused. "It's not that I want to die. I'm not particularly looking forward to that day. But there is no other way. No alternative."

"I'm not following you, Number Three," said Kitty. "No alternative to what?"

The Levi's Jesus hesitated for a second. "All of humanity is lost, eternally condemned unless a way is made, a way of escape.

"My father created each of you as the love of his life. You're his pride and joy. But something happened. A wedge was driven between you and him by sin. And sin is the one thing he can't stand—zero tolerance. Your sin and his perfection cannot coexist. He's repelled, repulsed by it. And because of that, judgment is sure." The panel squirmed.

"But—my father's love for you far exceeds his hate of sin. So he made a way. A way that he could take the judgment for your sin onto himself. Pay your debt."

A slight shiver passed through Jesus Number Three. "That's where I come into the picture. I'm the alternative. The way. The life that must be taken so that love may still be given. My mission is to offer myself as a sacrifice to cover the sins of the world. Every single sin of every last human being."

Kitty interrupted, "You're sounding awfully exclusive. Like there's only one way to God. One way to eternal life. One way to forgiveness. One truth."

"I—am—the way, the truth, and the life. As exclusive as it may sound, no one can come to the father except through me."

The producer was doing that hand-in-the-air circular-motion thing to let Jesus Number Three know that his time was up. Move it along—one minute left. Time to wrap it up.

The final questions were more basic. It was established that all three were thirty-two years old, right-handed, and had never sinned. They were all Capricorns and loved woodworking.

Then the announcer piped in, "And now, this word from our good friends at Oxydol. Getting your clothes whiter than white."

During the commercial break the triad of Christs fidgeted nervously. Eye contact was scarce. The studio audience murmured opinions with hushed conviction. Which one was he? They all had a certain believability to them.

Three, two, one.

"We're back. What a dilemma. Three Jesus Christs. Three hopes for humanity. Three symbols of faith. It's time to separate the wheat from the chaff, the sham from the man, the sinners from the Savior." Gary drew in a long, slow breath.

"Will the real Jesus Christ . . . please stand up."

There was the usual jockeying that took place. That stutter-standing bit. You know, milk the moment, prolong the suspense, draw it out as long as you can. Just as it looked as if one of the candidates was going to stand, for real, he just up and vanished. Disappeared into thin air. Poof!

This was certainly an interesting turn of events. Not something that happened every day here on set 3B. No precedent. Nothing had been rehearsed for a situation like this. Orson looked at Kitty. Kitty looked at Gary. Gary looked at Jesuses One and Two, who were both staring at the ceiling. Number Three had eighty-sixed. Vaporized. Vamoosed.

Twenty seconds deep into the quandary Gary regained his composure and stated, "Well, since we've, uh, only got one Jesus missing, we still have a pretty good chance that— the real one is still here."

He recued his line and reiterated his plea, "Will the real Jesus Christ please stand up."

The pair of Jesuses shook the shock out of their sandals and turned back to Gary with that "Are you serious?" look.

It only took Jesus Number Two one thin nanosecond to realize the magnitude of the opportunity that had just landed in his lap. Without missing a beat he slapped a paternal look of compassion across his face and rose out of his seat with smooth, hydraulic confidence.

For a second the crowd didn't know how to respond. Was he or wasn't he? Legit or hypocrite? Would they laud him or snub him?

A smattering of clapping erupted from the direction of the producer. In an instant the place blew sky-high with applause. From the looks of things, a halfhearted nudge was all that was needed for the whole gang to jump on the Jesus-Number-Two bandwagon.

Black-and-white had degenerated into shades of gray. Truth had become relative, scarce.

And in that instant, one Jesus retired, one Jesus started a new religion, and one Jesus, once again, went unrecognized.

The J. C. Cab Company

The cab was fairly nondescript—yuck yellow with the typical fender-bender scars earned from five years' worth of New York's asphalt insanity. The tires had a little less than the legal amount of tread remaining, but then, show me a New York cab with brand-new Michelins and I'll show you four stolen tires. The brown vinyl seats were the abused victims of a thousand overweight business butts; the springs had sprung and duct tape was making a valiant effort to prevent unwanted passenger acupuncture.

Jesus rode on one of those beaded seat-pad-cushion thingamajigs. He had an after-market leather-wrapped steering wheel, and an instrument panel complete with an array of nonworking idiot lights. The interior decor was appropriately topped off with a crucifix dangling from the rearview mirror.

This morning his cab was camped out in front of the Waldorf Astoria on Park and Fiftieth, the third cab in line. He turned on his Delco AM-only radio to a station that played his favorite Middle Eastern tunes. It made him homesick. He'd been in the states for five years now, but he still struggled with the language. Luckily, New York cab-drivers weren't really expected to speak the language.

His first fare of the day was a middle-aged man in a navy-blue business suit, as nondescript as Jesus' cab.

"Rockefeller Center, please," he said as their eyes met in the rearview mirror.

They pulled out and rode in silence for a few blocks when suddenly the man blurted out, "Jesus Christ?"

"Excuse me please?" said Jesus.

"It says on your meter that your name is Jesus Christ. Are you *the* Jesus Christ, the one from the Bible?"

"I am," was all Jesus said.

"So you're—like the Son of God and all that stuff?" His voice bore a hybrid concoction of curiosity and cynicism.

"Yes."

"This may seem like a silly question, but, uh, what are

you doing here, driving a cab? Shouldn't you be out saving the world, healing the sick, raising the dead?"

Jesus gave him a glance in the rearview mirror. By the creases around his eyes, the man in the back could see that this driver had sprouted a broad grin.

"Well, actually, I am doing every one of those things, each day," Jesus stated very matter-of-factly.

"Cool," the blue suit responded, then, "Hey, I don't suppose you could show me one of those tricks?"

The smile creases deepened. Jesus chuckled and said, "I prefer to calling them miracles, myself. I don't want to put down on Mr. David Copperfield, but his magic is not really so tricky. What we do isn't magic, it's more like . . . well . . ."

"We? Who's 'we'?"

"Oh, me and my father. We're kind of into this thing together. He is owned this cab company forever. My father is a real very good businessman. He saw a opportunity, saw that many of peoples seemed to be having trouble getting to places, you know, *really* getting to anywhere. So we begin this little business to helping them out."

"But, aren't you, like, the God incarnate guy—holy, omnipotent, and all that stuff? Why, then, would you start a cab company, and, and settle for just transporting people from one point to another?" For this Type A–personality

New Yorker the simplicity of this task seemed beyond comprehension.

Jesus continued, "A lot of people are just plain lost, looking really hard for direction . . . someone to say, 'Well, if you want to getting to Time Square you got to head down Park to Forty-Ninth, then west for a few blocks, and then a quick left on Seventh and voilà, there you are.' Everybody gets lost in New York City, so my father and me, we decide I should come down here and help people—lost people like you—get to where they're wanting to going."

"Well, Mr. Christ—number one, I'm not lost, and number two, I'm 'wanting to going' to Rockefeller Center." Mr. Blue Suit seemed to have abruptly tired of the conversation, his cynicism accelerating, leaving his curiosity at the curb. *Just another Big Apple kook,* he thought. Plus, Jesus was starting to get too close to home with all that "lost" talk. *Who does this pidgin-English, garlic-breathed immigrant think he's talking to? Lecturing me about direction. Huh! I'm a CEO, for Pete's sake. Giving direction is what I do. We CEOs always know where we're going, that's why we're CEOs. The nerve of this guy!*

As Jesus pulled curbside, the outwardly confident Armani suit exited with a toss of a two-dollar tip.

Before Jesus had time to flip on his blinker and pull out,

a thirty-fiveish woman rapped on the trunk, screamed dibs on the cab, and threw open the back door. Meredith tossed her laptop onto the backseat and fell through the door like she'd just slid into second.

Jesus turned and met her eyes just in time to see a dam of tears break the dike and pour down her seemingly innocent cheeks. Wanting to pose the more urgent question, Jesus simply asked, "Can I take you somewhere please, miss?"

After a couple of stuttered breaths she said, "Just drive. I'll figure out where later." Jesus pulled out without the usual I've-got-someplace-to-be-in-a-New-York-minute frenzy. Driving down Fifth, he glanced at her in the mirror. She didn't look like she was any nearer to ascertaining a direction for their trip. Sensing his stare and the imminent question, she said, "I don't know. You're the guy with the map. Why don't *you* tell me where I wanna go."

Finally. The response he loved. The reason he and his father had gotten into the taxi business in the first place. A lost rider—who knew she was lost—desperately looking for direction.

Jesus caught Meredith's eye in the mirror again. "Just sit backing and relax, enjoy the ride. I won't steer wrong for you. You're riding with the best cabby in all of New York City, the only driver in town who knows for really sure

where every road leads." What might have been an arrogant claim was delivered with the sincerest humility.
Simply stated truth. "These rides are so short, and most
people are so wrappinged up in busyness they forgetting
where is it they really want to going to. Trust me. I'll get
you where to you're going." He smiled at her, and then
with a believable reassurance and a playfulness in his voice
he said, "Things will be workinged out for good."

"Thanks Mr. . . ." She leaned over the seat to read his
name on the meter. "Mr. Christ." As she slouched in her
seat and dried her cheeks, she had the overwhelming sense
that she had, indeed, picked the right cabby—and the right
cab company.

God's Watering Hole

"Hey barkeep, gimme a drink."

If he had a nickel for every time he'd heard that phrase, he'd be a rich man. Filthy stinking rich.

They came in here by the droves, especially lately, seeking a sort of spiritual solace. Times were hard and life was complicated—a convincing provocateur to get people swilling from the bottle of truth.

This bar had become home to all types of cotton-mouthed patrons. Social drinkers, sophisticated sippers, discerning imbibers, and a whole gutter full of perpetual drunks; people who did shooters, shots, slammers, and basically used their faces as funnels for every brand of pain-relieving elixir known to man.

Some of the regulars never even came to drink. They came to see and be seen. A club mentality. People were the draw—who they'd meet and what they could do for them and to them. Networking.

Then there was always the occasional person who came because they were actually thirsty. A novel concept. This bartender especially liked these people. After all, he had the perfect drink for them. It was his own concoction . . . said it was the only truly thirst-quenching drink on the face of the earth. A pretty strong claim, even by bartenders' standards.

This, however, was not your typical corner bar. This watering hole was run by the man . . . I mean *the* man. This bar was owned and operated by God himself. Sole propri-etorship. And get this, he called his bar The Church. Yeah, I know. It sounded strange to me too. People saying, "Hey, you wanna meet down at The *Church* for drinks?" Or, "Man, I could really use a beer . . . let's go to The *Church.*" It just doesn't sound right, does it? But, it's his bar, I guess he can call it anything he likes.

Tonight was a typical Sunday evening at The Church. A middle-aged man had parked himself on his favorite barstool. The same one he sat on every single time he came in. (God thought it was funny how people got so attached to certain stools. It was like they owned them. And everybody knew it. "Hey, you can't sit there, that's Joe's stool." People were habitual little critters!)

God buffed a glass to an antiseptic sheen and set it in front of the new arrival. "What'll you have, Joe?" God seemed to know everybody by name. It was uncanny. "Can I interest you in my special concoction tonight?"

"Na. Just give me the regular." Joe's regular was a lite beer. Miller Lite, Bud Lite, any lite . . . every night. Night after night. A watered-down brew with just enough fire to keep him awake but not so much as to rouse him from his self-satisfied state of sedation.

Joe was a stool potato—a lazy, content-with-his-mediocre-life kind of guy, with a—how can I say this well, a lukewarm pathetic existence. Never too up. Never too down. Never wanted to try anything new. And he definitely never let anything God said or served affect him.

Joe was a pleasant enough guy around the bar. He talked with God every day . . . or should I say he talked *to* God every day. Told God his problems, complained to God about people that bugged him—do this, God . . . do that, God—it was pretty much a one-way diatribe.

He never really listened to God anymore. Too bad,

because God was a great shrinklike bartender. The kind that really warranted listening to.

More than anything else, though, God wanted to pour Joe a glass of his 100 proof concoction. But before God had ever opened this bar, he had decided that he would never force people to drink what they didn't want . . . or, at least what they didn't know they wanted. However, there were nights when Joe's lukewarmness really got to God and he was tempted to spit him right out the front door of the bar.

Suzanne always hung out by the door. She was another one of The Church members who got under God's skin. She was a nondrinker. Never seemed thirsty. It was like she was being satiated by another form of bubbly. Success.

Actually, bubbly pretty much described her too. A perky package with a closet full of designer style.

Suzanne saw The Church as her second office. Every "Hi there" was a business contact. Every "How ya doing?" was prelude to a sales pitch. "Wasn't the sermon great today . . . here's my card. Call me Monday."

There were lots of Suzannes. God didn't get it, how a person could be so parched and yet not want a drink. Inches from the well but miles from the water.

The Joes and Suzannes of The Church were bad enough,

but the clientele that really irked God were the perpetual drunks. They acted like sheep. Herd mentality. Huddled together. They spent way too much time at The Church. Always taking in. Drinking. Drinking. Drinking. What they needed was to leave The Church once in a while and go rub shoulders with the rest of the world. Sober up a little. Maybe stop drinking just long enough to take some of God's special concoction out there and share it with others. That was God's dream, his plan. But people seemed awfully content to sit on their barstools and drink themselves into a comatose stupor.

Yeah, the drunks were the worst. Ritualistic automatons. The means had become more important than the end. They worshiped the bottle, rarely ever talked with the bartender. And when they did, it was only to ask for another drink. It saddened God.

I often wondered why he didn't just up and sell the Church. Get rid of it. I mean, it obviously wasn't the successful business he had intended it to be. At times it was starting to look like just another bar . . . nothing special.

Suddenly, the catatonic calm of the bar was thrown into a three-alarm tizzy by a young woman bursting through the door. She was dressed far more casually than the average Church patron and was the immediate recipient of more than one disapproving stare. The Church wasn't used to getting people this fresh off the street.

Before God could even open his mouth, she leaned across the bar, looked him dead in the eye and declared, "I'm dying of thirst!" There was desperation in her tone. She was gasping for breath, like she'd arrived a scant two steps ahead of the fire of hell. "Give me something to drink! Please!"

"What would you like?" asked God. "Could I interest you in my own special . . ."

"You're the expert here! You tell me what you've got that can wash away a lifetime of thirst!"

God already had it poured and iced. And as he slid it across the bar to her he said, "Well, Kelly, I've got just the drink for you. One glass of this and I guarantee you'll never be thirsty again!"

Without taking time to question how he knew her name, she tipped the glass up all the way, guzzling as if her very life depended on it. The clear liquid overflowed the corners of her mouth and as it ran down her arms and dripped off of her elbows it seemed to calm and resuscitate her whole being. As she set the glass down she took a deep breath and collapsed onto a barstool. The look on her face held a new peace that wasn't there five minutes ago. She began conversing with God with an ease that belied their brief relationship.

The other patrons looked on with removed jealousy. They remembered a time when they, too, engaged in that easy-flowing conversation with this bartender; when they had tried his special concoction for the very first time. What an explosive taste sensation it had been.

Looking up, the Church regulars noticed Kelly heading for the door. *Leaving already? She'd just gotten there. Why such a big hurry?* Then they noticed she had something under her arm. It looked like a—a thermos. But what would she be doing with a thermos?

"Thanks, God!" she said, half running toward the door. "I know a lot of people out there who need this as badly as I did. This stuff is liquid gold!"

And through the closing door was heard, "Be back sooooooooon."

I guess that's why he doesn't sell the joint. The Church still serves up his special concoction. And on the out chance somebody bangs on the door, completely dehydrated, this lifesaving fluid is chilled and ready to be served.

God looked down the bar at another thirsty soul and with outstretched arms delivered his gracious invitation, "What'll you have, Bill? Can I interest you in my special concoction?"

CAUTION

If you haven't already done so, may I suggest you flip the book over and read your way back to the middle. Reading "Home" now may cause slight discoloration. And we don't want that.

So . . . save "Home" for last.

Home

Well, here you are. You've arrived at the middle of the book, where both ends meet—the cream of the Oreo.

Home.

You've read about a garbageman who does housecleaning, a hitchhiker who thumbed his way to earth, a bum who walked our streets so we could walk his, a cabdriver who instinctively knows the way home. All of these are pictures of God stepping into our world, making house calls, knocking on our doors. A God who became blue-collar for one reason . . . to bring us home.

Home.

You've read about being flown by the KiteMaster, resuscitated by the Tomorrow Tower fountain, warmed by Mr. Wellington's fire, and adopted by the mayor of True North. All of these are pictures of the long reach of love—a reach that stretches all the way from his home, his heart—to ours. This is a God whose white-collar shirttails can be ridden all the way home.

Home.

I love my home, almost everything about it. I love the driveway, how it bends to the left and then to the right, how you have to turn your head to keep the house in view. I love walking through the door—the smells so familiar. Soccer shoes, dog food, fireplace ash, Bounce fabric softener, berry-scented candles, and fresh brownies in the oven.

I love sitting on the deck early in the morning, watching the steam rise from the umbrella as the sun warms it. I love the contrast of our backyard cardinal, fluorescent-red against a forest of green.

I love the first time we eat on the porch in spring.

The first mowing of summer.

The first fire of fall.

The first snow day of winter.

I love sipping black-currant iced tea at the tail end of dinner as the girls regale me with stories of school, sports, and . . . boys. (Well, two out of three's not bad.)

I love that the phone isn't for me anymore, and that I don't have to spring up to answer it. There'd be no point, I'm not that quick—nobody is.

I love the sound of practicing piano, sizzling sausage, and the furnace kicking in. I love lighting pumpkins on Halloween and stringing garland at Christmas. I love the sound of a basketball on the driveway and playing H-O-R-S-E till way after dark. I love, "One more game, Dad?"

I love when homework's done early and dinners go late. I love tucking and tickling and hugging and praying. I love when the house is quiet and the only sound is the steady breathing of a home—at peace.

All those things I love. But there's more.

I love my wife. Mary. I always feel at home with her. She's the room that holds my heart. We've laughed and cried, we've fought and made up. We've been over, under, around, and through a lot of things together, but she's still the only girl I want to ask out. And the only thing I love more than going out with Mary, is coming home with her again.

I love our girls. They're the rhythm of our home—the tick in the clock, the current in the walls, the buzz in my ears . . . the hole in my pocket. Brianna, Lauren, and Taylor—they're masterpieces, some of the Artist's best work. He's graciously allowed me to hang all three originals on my walls for eighteen years or so, then he's going to take them on the road—give the rest of the world a chance to see them.

Oh yeah, then there's my dog, Strugs. A lovable mutt who would never turn down a ride in the car, but, just like us, Strugsy loves coming home again to her own dish, her own limbless Barbie doll, and her own tapestry-covered couch—which happens to double as ours, but it's hers when we're not around.

That's a peek into our home, the center of my Oreo. I bet I've got a million memories of things that have taken place between these walls—and I've only lived here for fourteen years. I've probably made it sound better than it really is, but sometimes—sometimes my home feels an awful lot like heaven.

And I've got a sneaking suspicion that heaven's going to feel an awful lot like home. I wouldn't be surprised if heaven has a driveway with a left and right jog in it, a basketball hoop in the turnaround, Christmas lights on the eaves, and brownies in the oven. I wonder how many memories I'll have of heaven after fourteen years?

Home.

I dream about the day my two homes will be married—the day my family checks in to heaven.

What a thought. My family, home.

Really home.

I don't know if Strugsy will be there, but if someone throws a stick in that direction I suspect she will be. I'll lean over a cloud and give a whistle. If she's within earshot she'll find her way home.

Sometimes I wonder where I'd be if I hadn't heard God whistling for me; if I had said, "Just a minute, there's a couple'a more cars I want to chase." The fact is, I do chase cars, still, more than I'd like to admit. But I know his whistle, and it always calls me home.

Home.

The Oreo has been split. You've eaten both cookies and you're standing on the creamy filling. You're home—I hope. Home is where I wanted you to end up.

From your vantage point, look back at the two sides you've just tasted.

God's blue collar. The singular purpose of his foray into our world—our closet—was to make a way to bring us back home. God with us.

God's white collar. Even now he's preparing that big walk-in closet in the sky—our real home—where we'll spend eternity with him. Us with God.

He needed to become a bum of sorts, to get dirt under his fingernails, for our sake. But there also had to be a dirt-free hand that could reach across time and pull this thing off.

One put himself in our place, the other placed himself in us. One made his home with us so the other could make his home, ours.

The plan required both sides of the cookie. It was never either/or. It was always both/and. Blue and white—or whatever metaphorical collars you choose—are the thump-thump of a heart that beats for us. The blood courses away from the heart and then it returns. It knows where home is. Jesus left his home, circulating life to us while God manned the pump. His heart is still pumping for us and won't stop till we're washed ashore on his doorstep.

Home.

If you have enjoyed this book by Terry Esau, consider these options.

The CD: Terry has written and produced a CD with 10 songs that are based on the stories from this book. The live, unplugged sound helps complete the story that the book has begun. Available through our Web site at www.FunkyJava.com. A great companion product to the book.

The Radio Show: It's called *Live At Funky Java*. Terry is in the process of producing a live, half-hour, weekly radio show that will feature him telling a story from this book as well as performing several songs. Think Garrison Keiller minus the folksy feel, and skewed a bit younger, edgier. Check the Web site for stations in your area.

The Web Site: www.FunkyJava.com. This is where you can order CDs, get info on the radio show, the book . . . and a bunch of other stuff about Terry and what he's up to. Also, look for the link to Terry Esau at the W Publishing Group Web site, www.wpublishinggroup.com.

Speaking engagements: In between his commercial music career and writing books, there's nothing that Terry loves more than traveling around telling his stories to people. If you've got a group that would like to book him for your event, call him at 952-476-2204, or email him at the address below.

E-mail Terry: Puddlehill@aol.com. He'd love to hear from you.

I've heard many people talk about the important things in their lives and then say, *"That's* what it's all about."

Well, here's my take on it.

Home.

That's what it's all about. God loves us so much that he wants to bring us home. Period.

I better run, I think I hear him whistling.

If you have enjoyed this book by Terry Esau, consider these options.

The CD: Terry has written and produced a CD with 10 songs that are based on the stories from this book. The live, unplugged sound helps complete the story that the book has begun. Available through our Web site at www.FunkyJava.com. A great companion product to the book.

The Radio Show: It's called *Live At Funky Java*. Terry is in the process of producing a live, half-hour, weekly radio show that will feature him telling a story from this book as well as performing several songs. Think Garrison Keiller minus the folksy feel, and skewed a bit younger, edgier. Check the Web site for stations in your area.

The Web Site: www.FunkyJava.com. This is where you can order CDs, get info on the radio show, the book . . . and a bunch of other stuff about Terry and what he's up to. Also, look for the link to Terry Esau at the W Publishing Group Web site, www.wpublishinggroup.com.

Speaking engagements: In between his commercial music career and writing books, there's nothing that Terry loves more than traveling around telling his stories to people. If you've got a group that would like to book him for your event, call him at 952-476-2204, or email him at the address below.

E-mail Terry: Puddlehill@aol.com. He'd love to hear from you.

White-Collar
GOD

Terry Esau

W PUBLISHING GROUP™

www.wpublishinggroup.com

A Division of Thomas Nelson, Inc.
www.ThomasNelson.com

White-Collar Contents

White-Collar God

To say he's successful would be quite an understatement. To say he has entrepreneurial inclinations would be stating the glaringly obvious. To say he's a big shot, a big wheel, a big deal, the big cheese, would be selling him short on "bigs."

The name embroidered on his white collar pretty much says it all . . .

God.

Think about it. His address? Heaven—it's about as white-collar as you can get. His staff numbers in the billions—that's enough to make any CEO's white collar turn

green. His portfolio? It makes Bill Gates's pile of green turn a pale shade of white. Yeah, his collar's white all right, blindingly white.

Virtually everything about him is bigger than life. He's not your ordinary, everyday, run-of-the-mill superhero. He can't be boxed in. He can't be packaged. He can't be defined. It's not just that he doesn't fit the mold—it turns out he is the mold. It's not just that he strays outside the lines—turns out he is the lines. He never had to climb the ladder—he is the ladder.

In *White-Collar God* you'll meet . . .

> God, the CEO of the Fire Factory.
> God, the architect of the Tomorrow Tower.
> God, the Big Is.
> God, the benevolent Mr. Wellington.
> God, the high-bidding portrait Artist.
> The ultramega Alpha and Omega.

These are the stories of a big God. The stories of a God who may have taken a ride on a train through a town called Mortality, but he didn't get off there. The route went on and so did he.

But let's back up a minute and check out that detour

through downtown Mortality. What was that all about? How do you reconcile that with this mysterious mighty Messiah? It's baffling, this flip side of the white-collared guru. Just when it seems this all-powerful leader ought to cinch up his tie a little tighter around his white collar, he flagrantly unbuttons his top button and shows us something completely contrary.

He shows us he's vulnerable. He shows us emotions that VIPs shouldn't show. We see an entourage that doesn't look very presidential. We see a carpenter who doesn't look very kingly.

That's the kicker. This white-collared king became smitten with a little peasant girl named Humanity. The God of everything—who could have had anything—came down with a "thing" for us. He could have snapped us like a twig, yet we were the very habit he couldn't break.

These are the stories of a mysterious God—one who measures the height of his love by the depth of his sacrifice. A God who wasn't afraid to not use force, to not command submission. He wanted the peasant girl, us, to love him for who he was, of our own free will. He became weak to show the might of his love. The prefect inverted the flow chart to demonstrate perfect love. It's not the standard MO for deities, but then he's never been the

poster child for "standard." He's never worn the "predictable" label.

This book is for people whose God has become manageable, definable, predictable. It's for people who haven't been surprised by God in a while. For people whose God never goes over fifty-five.

I suggest you buckle up.

These stories aren't all neat and clean, but neither is life. The symbolism may disturb you at times, but look beyond the images to the truths they represent. These aren't fairy tales, they're better than fairy tales, they're snapshots of truth. Pictures of God, fully engaged with humanity.

Get ready to stretch your imagination. Dare to see the God outside the lines, beyond the box. Prepare yourself for a God who's not your average, everyday run-of-the-mill superhero. His top button may be open, but there's no mistaking him. He's the one in the dazzling white collar.

The Fitting Room

To be honest, I've never trusted white collars all that much. They always seem to have an agenda up their sleeves. Yet, here I am about to step into a fitting room with a crisp white dress shirt under my arm. I can't help it. I need to see what it looks like on me, what it feels like.

This white shirt has made some pretty staggering claims. Says it can spiff me up, inside and out . . . make me look "perfect." If it's half that good, I'll be better dressed than I ever dreamed possible. Besides, what have I got to lose by trying it on? Like the salesperson said, "It doesn't cost to look."

Hey, why don't you join me? There's a rack of about ten shirts in the next few pages that might fit you pretty well. I

think you might like the look they give you. It could be a whole new you. Come on, let's upgrade our wardrobes. Mine could use it.

Oh, and when you're done here, head over to the Blue Fitting Room, if you haven't been there yet. They've got some really cool preworn denim shirts over there—the blue-collar variety. I have a feeling they're going to feel so natural you won't be able to resist going through the whole rack. After you've tried all of them on, meet me back here and we'll wear our new threads home. We'll blow everyone away with our new look, the new us.

If you need a couple of other sizes, just yell.

The Big Is

Once upon a time when cows could talk, a great debate took place. At the north end of the barn, all of us cows were beginning to gather around the trough. Tonight's topic was, *Which came first, the chicken or the egg?*

Fliers had been passed out in the yard announcing tonight's confab, and by the looks of things the attendance was not going to be disappointing. The barn was filled to the sills. The atmosphere, ripe with anticipation.

Stooley, a Longhorn and the undisputed stud of the farm, opened the proceedings. "Eh, eh, hem. OK, everyone, quiet down." Angus, a jet-black bull, banged his hoof against the sideboards to help silence the herd. Stooley continued, "As you know, this is part three in our series

relating to our feathered friends. Bessie, being the herd secretary, would you please read the minutes of our last two meetings?"

"It'd be my pleasure," said Bessie as she batted her eyes at Stooley. "Week one we bantered around the question of *McNuggets vs. Big Mac*. We all chose McNuggets for obvious self-preservation reasons, but expressed a great deal of consternation over the fact that ground beef should be labeled 'h-h-hamburger.' We decided it was a fairness issue, a great disservice considering the historical contributions we've made to 'h-h-hamburgers.'" She went on. "And last week, we had a very spirited discussion titled, *Roosters: Alarm Clocks or Annoying Cocks*. We all had rather strong opinions on that one too. We concluded that although the rooster is obnoxious, arrogant, and stinky, he still serves a useful purpose in society." She batted her big browns, swished her tail and said, "Thus ends the reading of the minutes."

"Thank you, Bessie," said Stooley, slightly embarrassed by her flirtatiousness. He moved on. "Well, we finish this series with tonight's topic. It's one that has buffaloed me for years. But first, a disclaimer. I'd like to say that I am personally acquainted with several chickens here in the yard, some with whom I'm on a first-name basis; friends, if you

will. However, my relationships with eggs are—considerably more limited at this point." We chuckled in the back row. "That being said, I don't think we should allow our friendships with the chickens to skew our discussion. The egg deserves its day. So, let us not speak derogatorily of eggs . . . or chickens. Those are the ground rules. Fair enough?" A hundred hooves clopped in unison.

"Very well then, I should like to start by posing the question of preexistence. The chicken or the egg—which is the predecessor? Anyone?"

"When you say preexisted, exactly what do you mean?" said one brown-and-white heifer as she swished at a fly with her tail.

"Well, have you ever seen a chick hatch from anything other than an egg?" interjected a plain-brown cow. "The egg simply must precede the chicken."

"Hogwash!" bellowed an intellectual old Hereford tossing in his cud's worth. "Your argument is full of cracks." He swayed his head back and forth as he talked. "Who in this barn has ever seen a chicken egg appear from nothing?" He looked around. "Anyone?" No response. "Who in this barn has ever seen a chicken egg grow from—from the dirt?" He raised his head. Mumbled lowing. "Who in this barn has ever laid an egg?" A few of us in

the back row snickered. "There you have it, a chicken must exist in order for an egg to exist. That is the physics of eggs." The Harvard Hereford arrogantly lifted his muzzle to the sky.

Shirley, the plain-brown cow, wasn't about to go down that easily. She fired back, "Your theory, too, is flawed. Completely hard-boiled if you ask me. Egg shells are impervious. What's in is in, and what's out is out. Chickens don't swallow magic shrinking pills and then burrow their way into eggs. There's no hocus-pocus shell game going on. The egg is exited from the inside out. The chicken comes from the egg. The egg came first!"

A cool old cow with a piece of grass hanging out of her mouth tossed in her two cents. "Hey, Shirley, let me ask you this. Did your calf birth you or did you birth your calf?" More cud-chewing chuckling from the back row.

The discussion went on. We got a little off track and debated the taste of eggs vs. chickens. We decided it must be a tossup, since the farmer ate both. Of course, come to think of it, the farmer ate almost everything on the farm, including us. We detoured and passed a resolution declaring the farmer inhumane. We basically do that at least once every time we get together.

Back to chickens, one cow suggested that maybe the

gizzard was the key to the whole question, since nobody knew what it was or what it did. "Maybe the gizzard came first!"

Stooley, getting a bit put out by the randomness and lack of direction in the herd, threw out, "OK, last chance. Does an-y-bo-dy have anything insightful to say regarding our topic?"

One of the cows, whose mother and father had been brother and sister, spoke up. "I—I ate a chicken egg once . . . had me plenty worried, it did. Thought I might give birth to a chicken. But nuttin' ever came of it, thank goodness. That woulda sure been a tough one to 'xplain to the bull."

Stooley rolled his eyes. "Thank you for sharing, Bertha." The discussion was going nowhere.

Just then, a wise old hen perched on the window sill cleared her throat with a muffled "doodle doo" sound. She had been sitting there all evening, taking in the whole debate. No longer able to tolerate this barnyard nonsense, she clucked in with, "Well I never heard such foolishness. Chickens and eggs—and cows, for that matter—don't just hatch out of thin air. There's gotta be a *someone, somewhere* before a *something* can happen. That's just plain old horse sense."

"Well I, for one, have never seen this 'someone' you're talking about," responded the Ivy League bovine. "If there is a 'someone,' then how come no one has ever seen him?"

The hen cocked her head and thought for a second, then said very matter-of-factly, "There's a fly on your behind. Can you see it? Mmm?" The Hereford started to swing his head around then stopped, realizing he was being suckered into attempting the impossible. The hen continued, "Just because you can't see the fly on your buttocks doesn't mean it's not there. You'll feel him soon enough.

"Furthermore . . ."

Without warning the hen leaped from the sill and flew acrobatically over the heads of the cows and landed squarely on the nose of the Hereford. He locked up all four knees to keep from staggering with surprise.

The hen leaned forward and looked the cow right in the eyes and said, "Correct me if I'm wrong, but I believe I've seen you in the pasture, leaning across the electric fence trying to sneak a nibble of the farmer's corn. Mmmm?" The cow sheepishly gandered up toward the ceiling. "Well, when you felt that jolt smack you in the old snout, tell me, did you see the electricity?"

"Mmmmmnnno."

"So, let's review. We've established that some things exist that can't be seen. Real, but not visible. But, that still doesn't answer our question: Which came first? Here's how I see it." She fluffed her feathers, using her wings to gesture. "Something that isn't can't become something that is, unless that which is precedes that which isn't. Now, the isn'ts, that's us. You and me, we used to be isn'ts. But the Big Is decided to—hatch us. And that's when we left isn'tville and became little is's.

"You may ask, and logically so, where did the Big Is come from?" She laughed. "I can't explain that. How could I? Back then, when Is already was, I was still an isn't. We all were." She raised the point of her wing in the air. "But— the Big Is never was an isn't. He couldn't have been."

The prep-school Hereford chipped in with, "Because an is can't hatch from an isn't." The Ivy League side of beef was beginning to catch on; his brain was tenderizing.

"Precisely. The Is always was."

Lots of lowing, nodding, and swishing.

Stooley summarized, "So what you're saying is, everything and everyone was an isn't?"

"Right."

"Pigs were isn'ts?" asked the plain-brown cow.

"Yup."

"Dogs?"

"Yup."

"Cars?"

"Isn'ts."

"Uh . . . milk machines?" asked a pregnant cow.

"Isn'ts."

Bertha stepped forward again and in a pardon-me-for-living drawl asked, "Well, uh, I was just a' wonderin', w-w-was the farmer an isn't?"

"Especially the farmer!" blurted out the hen as she did a three-sixty with a double twist in the air, landing on the head of Stooley. The whole barn erupted in a cheer. Her high-pitched cluck intensified with the passion of conviction. "The Big Is always was. Before barns and electric fences, before butchers and supermarkets, before delis and McDonald's, before Ruth's Chris Steak House, before Stuart Andersons, before chickens and eggs. He's bigger, he's better, he's brighter. The Is was before and I'm guessin' the Is will be after. The Is is here, the Is is there, the Is is everywhere. The Is just plain is . . . and always was." The hen got this cocky look on her face and punched out her last line, "I'm tellin' you cows, isn't it wonderful that the Big Is never was an isn't but always was an Is! Isn't that just the best news you ever heard?"

She started doing a little chicken dance on Stooley's
head and sang this squawky melody.

My God's not a chicken
I doubt he's a cow
Not likely the farmer
Good heavens, no sow

He's gotta be bigger
Than a silo or two
There's a good chance he's brighter
Than me and you

I know without doubt
I won't figure it out
Cuz if'n I could
He'd be less—than—he—should—

Oh—I ain't no genius
But I'm bettin' he is
Chickens and eggs
The plans were his

Buck, buck, b, b, buck
Buck, buck, buck, buck, buck . . .

The wise old hen danced on. A few of us cows even joined in. Mooing, swaying, swishing, chewing . . . it was oddly musical in a barnyard sort of way.

We never did figure out which came first. But then, we're cows. How could we? My guess is the hen had it right; there's gotta be a someone somewhere before there can be a something. Seems to make sense. I think I'm just gonna hang out and keep an eye peeled for Someone . . . the Big Is. And when I see him, I'll ask him which came first. And for this cow, that'll settle it.

Well, gotta go. My hooves are killin' me. See ya later.

February Fire

My fire went out in November. It's not that I ran out of wood, or paper, it's more like I ran out of—well, fire. I still had everything I needed to make a fire—all the ingredients, but something was missing, the something that makes heat, warmth. I couldn't find it and didn't even know where to look for it.

When I think about it now, my fires had never been much to brag about. It's not that they didn't look fireish, but they always had a showroom quality to them . . . more pizazz than essence. They had sparkle to burn, but no blaze to warm. They cast shadows, but couldn't throw heat.

At first I was OK without heat, as long as the fire burned big and bright. If the fire was flashy enough I could almost

talk myself into feeling the warmth. But gradually, even the imagined heat escaped up the chimney. That's when the cold became real—when the chill entered my home. One day I sat down in front of my fire and saw it for what it was . . . anemic strands of pale, passionless flame. I hardly recognized it; it seemed artificial, hollow. And I was cold.

For the next month I did everything in my power to coax my hearth to life. I went through boxes of matches, stacks of papers. I created sparks without fire, flames without heat. I tried burning a lot of different things that made some pretty hot claims, but they all left me cold.

In the evening I would go for walks, long walks. I'm not sure if it was an attempt to close my eyes to my predicament or if I just wanted to see what other people's houses looked like—houses that harbored real fires. My favorite walk took me by the Wellington Mansion. It was the original house in Bakersville, the oldest house. The centerpiece of our little town. It was over a mile from my house, but worth every step. The place glowed, practically radiated heat. Mr. Wellington had fire, lots of it. I think I counted twelve chimneys and there were fires in at least half of them at all times.

I remember walking by there for weeks, slowing as I went by, watching the smoke curl from the chimney tops.

I walked downwind so I could smell it. I climbed the drifted snowbanks so I could look in and see the firelight flickering against the walls. It was a study in light. I imagined the warmth on my skin, my face.

Every day I fought the urge to approach the front door, ring the bell and invite myself in. I had heard that Mr. Wellington was a kindly old gentleman, generous with strangers, but I'd never met him personally. I couldn't just waltz up to his door and expect him to drop everything and give me a tour. It seemed so presumptuous, so I walked on by. Again.

One night, I told myself I'd just walk up to the door. I wouldn't ring the bell, I'd just get close. I climbed the last four stairs, hands in my pockets, trying to look casual, inconspicuous. There was a big Welcome mat in front of the door and an engraved bronze plaque attached to the wall that said, "Make Yourself at Home." Maybe it was the plaque, maybe it was the wind, but I involuntarily reached for the bell. I felt the button go in as I pushed it. I actually thought about running, but I had crossed the invisible line and now I had to stay. I hurriedly stumbled through a mental rehearsal for why I was ringing the bell. The explanation seemed so clumsy in my mind I dreaded hearing it trip out of my mouth.

When no one answered I was almost relieved. I noticed the inner door was slightly ajar, an inch or so. Another freak inoculation of bravery punctured my right arm. I knocked on the door, surprisingly hard. Still nothing. Feeling very cold and having spent so much courage just getting to this point, I pulled the storm door open a foot and yelled through the opening, "Hello. Anybody home?" No response. All I could hear was the crackling of the fire in the next room. I stepped just inside the door, wondering where this dose of courage had come from. "Excuse me. Um, I was just wondering if, uh, if it would be all right with you if I came in and just, um, stood by your fire? Just for a minute or so?" Still nothing. "Anyone?"

I started to feel ill at ease, not to mention uninvited, and I turned to leave. Just then a loud snap from the fire reminded me of my chill. I turned back and looked around the foyer. A beautiful chandelier hung above me with a thousand glowing crystalline pendants. A wide arcing staircase of maple and cherry lay straight ahead of me. It ascended counterclockwise to a balcony lined with heavily framed landscape paintings. The walls were a mix of mahogany trim and deep burgundy paint.

The fire snapped again. I made a mental calculation . . . if I took two considerable steps straight ahead, I should be

able to look into the living room and see the fire. *Why not,* I thought, *I'm this far in.* I took those two giant steps and turned to face the room. I felt the warm glow on my face before I had even finished the turn.

The fire captured me. There was an instantaneous feeling of connection with something that had been missing, absent, lost. I felt a surge of emotion—at first I thought it was fear—but I knew it was more than just that. Not sure how to handle this avalanche of feelings, I turned and ran out the door.

I was still warm when I arrived home that night. I made a hot cup of tea and sat down in my big soft chair in the living room. I tried to picture what else had been in that room with the fire, but I realized I hadn't even looked at anything else. I had a vivid mental picture of the entryway, but the living room? Nothing. The fire had so consumed me that its presence was my only memory—nothing else had even registered.

As I sat in my chair, reliving the evening, something caught my attention. I thought I smelled something. Smoke. I jumped up and started checking around the house. Was something burning? I looked everywhere, upstairs and down . . . nothing. I came back to the living room. There it was again, a faint smell of smoke. I finally figured it had to

be coming from one of the neighbors' houses and let it go at that. I closed my eyes, picturing Mr. Wellington's fire, and fell fast asleep.

The next night I walked again. There were chunky snowflakes falling through the evergreens in front of the Wellington Mansion. The light sifted through the windows and danced on the floating white crystals. The warm pull was irresistible. Without hesitation, I walked up to the door and rang the bell.

Again there was no answer. I rang twice and waited. I noticed the stately wooden door was even further ajar tonight; it was practically swung open. Something else was new. There, stuck to the bronze plaque, was a handwritten note. In graceful penmanship it simply said, "Please, come on in. Make yourself completely at home."

So, he had seen me last night. I wondered why he hadn't come down, said "Hi"? Had he been watching me the whole time? I stepped inside the door.

"Hello? Mr. Wellington?" I kicked the snow off my shoes as I waited for a response. "You have a beautiful place here." I took another step in. "Would you mind terribly if I just warmed myself by your fire for a minute or two again? I won't be long." The only sound was the crackling of the fire. I followed it into the living room.

It was everything I had remembered. Every inch of the hearth flashed with flames. Several good-sized logs lay on a gleaming bed of coals. The logs looked like they had been freshly laid on the fire. Had Mr. Wellington seen me coming? Had he refreshed the fire just for me?

I walked closer to the fire this time—halfway across the living room. The warmth saturated me immediately. I felt a droplet of water land on my nose as the fire melted the snow on my hair.

I reached my hands toward the fire, receiving its warmth, pulling it toward me. My muscles relaxed. My breathing slowed. The heat almost seemed to be erasing the months I'd spent without fire. The flames touched me in a healing way, in places I never knew needed healing.

Who is Mr. Wellington? What kind of man invites a perfect stranger into his home? The kind of man who knows how to make a fire, that's who, I thought, answering my own question. As I left that night I yelled from the entryway, "Thanks, Mr. Wellington. Thanks for sharing your fire."

As soon as I opened my front door I knew something was different. The smell of smoke was much stronger than it had been last night. I put my sleeve up to my nose, thinking maybe it was just my clothes that had taken on the smell from Mr. Wellington's fire, but I knew—I knew that

wasn't it. As I rounded the kitchen and headed for the living room, I saw the glow. The room was bathed in a faint amber tint. Subtle, but certain. I stopped at the edge of the room and peaked around the corner toward the fireplace. I couldn't believe what I saw. It was beautiful. There was no fire, but the hearth was covered with embers, a bed of red-hot coals. The room had a warmth it hadn't enjoyed for months. My home was coming back to life.

It didn't make any sense, this rekindling, but yet it seemed completely natural. I couldn't explain it, but almost felt like I didn't need to. Back in November I had ignited all kinds of things on my own and never produced a heat I could feel. This new beginning felt real. I didn't question this discovery, I was enjoying it too much to question it.

The next evening I was even more eager to pay my nightly visit to the mansion. Things were turning around for me and, in large part, it seemed due to my new acquaintance with Mr. Wellington and his fire.

This night as I skipped up the walk I noticed another note hanging on the door. It said, "I enjoyed your visit last night. Please feel free to stay as long as you like, till you're warm. Try out my chair. I moved it in front of the fire just for you."

I did. This was the closest I had been to the fire yet. The

chair had been pulled around squarely in front of the hearth. I fell into it and was surprised how it fit me . . . like it was my chair, custom built for me. I took my shoes off and stretched my legs toward the fire. I was sitting in a stranger's house, and yet I was completely comfortable, completely at home. It felt so right.

I stared into the fire for hours that night, mesmerized by the blue, red, and yellow flames. They seemed to talk to me. They told me of where I'd been and where I was going. They showed me who I was and who I could be. I saw ashes of failure fall and sparks of hope rise. The chimney carried the sparks heavenward and sprinkled them across the sky. I had a sense that I had been freed, lifted and released by the fire; the darkness lifted, the chill released. I snuggled down into the leather chair and fell asleep under a peaceful blanket of warm.

The sun was just beginning to flirt with the horizon when I woke up. I'd been there all night. I was toasty, my cheeks rosy red. I sprang from the chair with an excitement I hadn't had in . . . well, ever. I threw on my shoes and ran out the door. Halfway down the walk I skidded to a stop, wheeled, and ran back inside. With a lilt in my voice I said, "I still haven't stayed as long as I'd like, but I'm getting there. Thanks, Mr. Wellington—see you tonight."

As I started jogging toward home, my mind jumped from his fireplace to mine. Would my coals be even brighter, hotter? I notched it up a few miles per hour. As I ran down the middle of the road, skipping over the long shadows of dawn, I felt the steam coming off my heat-saturated body. Would the glow still be there? Anticipation coaxed me into a full-out sprint. Did I dare to wish for fire? I practically flew around the last corner, sprinting down to the end of the block. I pulled up abruptly and stood, staring, in the middle of the street.

Through the steamy mist of my own frozen breath I gazed toward my house. My eyes passed over it the first time, thinking they had focused on the wrong three-bedroom English Tudor. My eyes shifted one lot back. My knees gave a quiver as I realized it was my house that was aglow, it was my windows that were ablaze, it was my chimney that was puffing like an industrial smokestack.

I did the last hundred in ten flat. I threw the door open and skittered across the hardwood floor, sliding the last few steps into the living room. Before I could even look, the snap-crackling told the story. It was an inferno, the biggest fire my hearth had ever seen; not just sparkle and flash, but sizzle and fizz. It was throwing strikes of pure heat. It was real, the fire was real. The snap was familiar, the warmth

reminiscent of a fire I had come to know. Mr. Wellington's fire had come home . . . to my home.

I spent the day in a dreamland. I knew this dream was reality, but reality had never felt this good before. I had never spent an entire day barefoot . . . and warm, in winter. I danced around in a T-shirt. I ate frozen yogurt and drank iced tea. My house was so hot, I even left my front door ajar.

I had heat to spare.

At about seven o'clock that night I grabbed my coat and gloves and headed for the front door. Even though I had my own fire now, I was still drawn to Mr. Wellington's . . . maybe even more so *because* I had my own fire. It's hard to explain.

As I pushed the front door open I ran headfirst into a woman standing on my steps. I grabbed at her arm just in time to keep her from falling off the steps into my shrubs.

"Oh, oh, I'm sorry," I said. "I didn't see you there. Are you OK?"

She was even more startled than me. Flustered and confused . . . and embarrassed. "You must think I'm a snoop. I'm not, really, I'm just . . ."

"No, that's OK, you just startled me," I said, trying to downplay the whole situation. Whoever this woman was, we were getting off to an awkward start.

Finally, I looked at her, in the eyes. She was a middle-aged woman, with eyes that looked sad. She was looking down at her feet when she decided to speak. "I'm really sorry, but I was just, well . . . I'll, I'll come back later . . . you're leaving so, I'll just come back . . ." she trailed off as she turned to leave.

"No," I said. "I'm in no huge rush. What can I do for you, Miss . . . ?"

"Jen, Jennifer. I live two doors down. Right over there." She pointed.

"Hi, Jennifer. I thought you looked familiar." Then I added, "You look—cold. How long have you been out here?" She paused. "A while."

It seemed like she was trying to figure out what to say. She finally found some momentum, "You'll probably think I'm nuts, but I've been looking at your house all day. Your windows . . . they're glowing. I noticed your chimney . . . it's busy." We both smiled. "Well, you've obviously got a fire in there and, well, uh, my fire went out a while back, and, I was just wondering if, if I could . . ."

" . . . come in and stand by my fire?" I finished her question for her. She looked like she was caught between a smile and tears. I grabbed her hand and started pulling her into my house, then stopped.

"Wait a minute," I said. "I've got an even better idea. Wanna see the best, most beautiful fire in the world?" I didn't wait for her answer, I just started tugging her down the street. As she bounced along beside me I told her my story, which I suspected would soon be her story. Just hearing about this fire was bringing a little color back to her cheeks. I wondered if she had any idea how this fire would change her life.

Well, that's how I found fire . . . for real. Good story, huh? If you're ever in Bakersville, make sure you visit the Wellington Mansion. You really need to experience it . . . this fire.

Anyhow, I haven't figured it all out yet, but one thing I do know . . . I was cold but now I'm warm. It's February, and I've got a new fire burning in my home.

God On-Line

Yesterday I signed on to check my e-mail. You gotta love those four little words:

Welcome. You've got mail.

Today I wasn't disappointed. Tons of mail. Ninety-eight percent junk, but mail just the same. Cyberspace has become the postal route of a 56K electronic Cliff Claven . . . you know, "Neither rain nor sleet—solar static nor power surges will keep it from its appointed rounds."

Before I signed off I glanced up at the "AOL *Today*" highlights and noticed something quite odd. Under an icon of

an old man was the title "Q & A time with God in *Goin' Up* chat room. 8 to 9 P.M. tonight."

Being the curiosity seeker that I am, I surfed on over to check it out. God on-line? Go figure. Must be a scam, a publicity stunt. Still, who can resist.

The conversation was already in high gear . . .

THOTPOLICE: so you're saying there are absolutes? who believes that anymore?

GOD: Me.

JACKJAY: Well, aren't we mister politically INcorrect.

GOD: Incorrect, no. Political—definitely no.

MISTER6: HEY, WHAT'S THE DEAL WITH THE VIRGIN BIRTH? WHO CAME UP WITH THAT?

GOD: Me.

THOTPOLICE: couldn't you have just beamed yourself down?

SPACELEE: Or morphed into adulthood . . . skip all that messy stuff.

GOD: I wanted to experience true humanity. All of it.

MISTER6: SO YOU'RE SAYING YOU WERE BORN ONE OF US, LIVED ON EARTH, FELT PAIN, HUNGER, LONELINESS?

GOD: Yup.

MISTER6: WHY?

GOD: Why do you think?

FRATRAT: Not this again. You always were the king of answering a question with a question.

GOD: Really? How's that make you feel?

FRATRAT: @#*%!

STANBEE: I seen billy Graham on tV talk about you.

THOTPOLICE: SAW!!!

GOD: I like Billy. We're pretty close.

STANBEE: He said you came to earth becuz you love people.

PINGLITE: Spell much?

THOTPOLICE: Yale-boy!

GOD: I do. I can't help myself. I look at you and I see my children.

THOTPOLICE: yo, dad. i need a new car. if you love me so much break out that supernatural visa card! let's earn you some frequent-flyer miles, buddy!

PINGLITE: Hey, I already got a stepdad. I don't need another one.

GOD: I had a stepdad too. A carpenter. We didn't always agree either. We were pretty different—of course, I could say that about everybody.

STANBEE: How can you lovE me? you don't know me.

THOTPOLICE: stanbee, you loser. he DOESN'T love you, you stupi . . .

PINGLITE: Hey, THOTPOLICE, what happened? Where'd you go?

GOD: I think he's having some computer problems. Modem's on the fritz.

SKATEBORED: Are you married, God? What's Mrs. God look like? Where do you go to meet chicks?

GOD: I've known you forever, Stan Blackford. Before you were born I knew you, I loved you.

SKATEBORED: Maybe she's a Ms. God . . . has her own career and everything. Got a "Sim Universe" of her own to manipulate.

DIPORT: IS THIS REALLY GOD?

GOLDIE: Ralph, it's you, isn't it? This isn't God. If you were the real God you wouldn't be wasting your time with us.

STANBEE: Why DO you waste your time with us? we're just a bunch oF sinners.

GRETCHUP: Speak for yourself, gutter mind.

GOD: Hey, sinners are my favorite people. When I was on earth I hung out with them. Besides, they're the ones who need me, or should I say the ones who know they need me. And besides, time is not a big deal to me. Forever

is enough time to get most things done, at least the things I really want to do.

SKATEBORED: Does Ms. God nag you like my wife? I suppose if you say "To the Moon, Alice" you can really send her there. COOL!! Could you teach me how to do that?

ALEXGYM: HAVE YOU EVER HAD A REALLY GOOD BURRITO, GOD? CAN YOU GET GOOD MEXICAN IN HEAVEN? CAUSE IF YOU CAN'T I'M NOT SURE I WANT TO GO THERE.

GOD: Who do you think invented salsa? If you make it to heaven, believe me, you will not be disappointed in the cuisine.

ALEXGYM: IF? WHAT-D-YA MEAN, IF?

SKATEBORED: Yeah. Ms. God wouldn't leave me here, would she?

GOD: Check out your Bible, the book of John. It's really pretty clear in there.

WHOZIT: Bible schmible. A bunch of fables, bedtime stories for kids.

GOD: Really? I always thought it was—inspired.

STANBEE: Uh, God? How'd you know my last name.

ALEXGYM: HEY, STAN. IS YOUR LAST NAME BLACKFORD?

STANBEE: Yeah.

WHOZIT: Member profile search.

STANBEE: I didn't fill out my member profile.

GRETCHUP: Lucky guess.

A-TOM: Hey, God. Tell me my last name and I'll think about believing in you.

SKATEBORED: Yeah, what's my grandmother's sister's mother's cousin's aunt's maiden name, mister know-it-all?

GOD: Do you honestly think it would be harder for me to come up with that name than to create the whole universe out of nothing?

STANBEE: I believe in you, god.

A-TOM: Oh boy. I'm tearing up . . . it's so touching.

SKATEBORED: Where's a cybertissue when you need one?

STANBEE: I mean it. I want to know you.

A-TOM: This is turning into a tearjerking chick flick.

GOD: I see our time is up. It was fun chatting with you all.

STANBEE: Where are you going? Please don't leave me.

GOD: I won't leave you. Everywhere you go you'll find me. You don't need to go on-line to talk with me. I've been on-line forever. Pre-Internet. Pre-AOL. We can talk anytime. Anywhere. Just think it and I'll be there. Bye-bye. I love you all . . . I really do.

DELORE: WHO WAS THAT?

A-TOM: I don't know. Kinda gives me the creeps.

SKATEBORED: Hey, Stan. You there?

SKATEBORED: Stan Blackford?

The Painting

It appeared to be an art auction for the mob. Shady-looking characters puffing on Cuban cigars. Tuxedoed bodyguards hovering over zoot-suited dons. Women draped in long wigs and longer fur coats. A Doberman leashed to a rhinestone collar. Shabby chic meets Mafioso vogue.

The seedy underbelly of the art world had congregated in an old abandoned warehouse. Metal folding chairs were aligned with haphazard symmetry. A makeshift stage had been constructed of pallets and crates. The setting sun streamed through the thirty-five-foot-high windows ringing the warehouse ceiling, casting shadowy silhouettes on the concrete floor. One beam of light landed squarely on an easel that held the painting, the centerpiece of today's

auction. The easel was crudely constructed of a loose support timber with a two-by-four nailed horizontally in the middle. The painting rested precariously on the two-by-four, shrouded in purple velvet. Just to its left stood an old podium with a gavel lying crossways on top, ready to call the mob to action.

I didn't know how or why I was there. I knew nobody and nobody seemed to know me. I sat in the front, facing the crowd, and yet I seemed virtually invisible. They looked at me, but didn't really see me.

The entire crowd rose to its feet as a squatty man with a skinny mustache approached the podium. He had a red silk handkerchief flamboyantly displayed in his lapel pocket and a tie bar that looked to be a replica of an AK-47. It was restraining a fiery red Jerry Garcia tie that was considerably louder than the crowd.

As he set his bowler hat on the podium, all the guests placed their right hands over their hearts in a sort of fraternal salute. Then all the suits took their seats. He spoke.

"OK, you'se all know why we're here, so let's get started. My name is Vito and dis here's the painting you'se all wanna get y' hands on. Mario?" He nodded to a goon-like character, and Mario neatly pulled the velvet from the painting and stepped down from the pallets.

The room suddenly became brighter, and now I felt rather conspicuous on stage. If I could have, I would have run, but I seemed to be frozen in place. I decided to hold my position and avoid eye contact.

Vito pulled a sheet of paper from his lapel pocket, put on a pair of reading glasses, and began to read his description of the painting.

"Dis painting is a portrait of an ordinary man like Mario, or Steffanno, or you, Roberto. But the painting ain't ordinary, you'se can see dat. It's beautiful—really, really nice. And I know all of you'se know the Artist. You know dat he's the best that ever was or ever will be. Der's no question about dat. Sure, I know he and I, we have our differences, you'se all know dat, too, but dat don't take away from the fact dat dis is still a masterpiece painted by the master Artist."

He continued, "Now—I know dat dis painting has seen some rough days. Yeah, it's got some scratches, some smudges . . . a couple a bullet holes." He laughed to himself. "Dis fella lived a careless life, but den who's of us in dis room hasn't, right?" Muffled laughter. "So's it's got a rip or two, 'at don't matter, it's still a one-of-a-kind original, and you'se all know it. So, let's start the bidding at one hundred thousand."

There was a slight pause, then some snickers. Then the snickers turned to laughter, and the laughter became a roar. The walls of the warehouse ricocheted with crazy hoots and hollers until Vito finally pulled a pistol from his jacket pocket and fired it into the air. This fearless crowd, so accustomed to gunfire, barely paid any attention to Vito until he emptied the entire clip into the ceiling.

A tall, sophisticated gentleman holding the leash of the Doberman stood and faced Vito. He was still struggling a bit to restrain his laughter when he began to speak. "With all due respect, surely you jest, Vito. I mean, look at this painting! It's a mess. It's frayed, it's torn," he chuckled. "It's lived a hard life. Quite frankly, I'm a little surprised you even called us together for this." He sat down.

The mumbling began building again until a woman in a mink coat yelled out, "I'll give you five bucks to take it off your hands."

Another man yelled, "Five and a quarter," without taking the cigar out of his mouth. The room was starting to enjoy this little game. A man with a patch over his eye bellowed, "'At's a pretty nice frame, uh, I'm feelin' generous today—how's about ten dollars?"

The place erupted in laughter again. The bidding became a form of one-upmanship. Vito, having spent all of

his ammo on the first outburst, was left with only his gavel to restore order.

He was pounding the podium to splinters when the back door of the warehouse opened, causing an attention-grabbing beam of light to strafe the crowd. I couldn't see who it was; the sunlight was wrapped around him, leaving our eyes with nothing but a profile. A few dozen hands in the room had reached into their pockets and were finger-ing the triggers of their Saturday-night specials. The man took several steps forward. Each footfall silenced the crowd far more than Vito's gunshots ever had. Now, the only sound was leather on concrete and the echoes it created.

As he reached the back of the aisle he stopped. From my vantage point I could see he was an elderly gentleman, very well dressed, with a crook-topped cane in his right hand. He looked far more dignified than the rest of the crowd, and something about him seemed familiar. As he took off his hat he said, "Hello, Vito."

Vito seemed to squirm a bit at the sound of his voice. "Sir," was all he could come out with.

"I see you're auctioning off my painting. I don't recall ever selling this piece."

I saw Vito's hand nervously wiggling in his pocket, scrounging around for some loose courage. He knew he'd

have to answer that charge but he decided to deflect some of the attention until he could gather his wits.

"Uh, ladies and gentlemen, I suspect you all know dis already, but dis here is the Artist himself. We're honored to have you here, sir." He took a couple of shaky breaths, dropped another coin in the courage slot and continued. "What you say is true. This piece never was for sale, but because of, shall we say, extenuatin' circumstances, it seems to have fallen into my hands." Vito's confidence meter was reading stronger every second. He looked over at me and continued, "What was I to do? This little 'portrait man' here seemed to enjoy his place on my wall more than he did on yours." Then, chuckling, "I guess he liked the personal accouterments of my den more than yours. No harm done. You win some, you lose some, huh? So's anyhow, have a seat, sir, you're welcome to bid for da painting just like everybody else. OK?"

The Artist didn't respond. He just took a handkerchief from his pocket, brushed the dust from a chair, and sat down.

The bogus auction continued, although now, no one seemed to be willing to ridicule the work as before. With the laughter held in check the bids reached four figures, still several zeros shy of its appraised worth.

Everyone was expecting the Artist to bid on the painting. After all, the price was low and he definitely had the appearance of wealth, yet he sat in silence. The activity diminished and the crowd began to grow restless.

Vito, sensing the end, jumped in, "So's we got a bid of one thousand, three hundred. Any of you'se out der wanna up dat?"

Nothing.

The Artist, visibly discouraged by the proceedings, pushed off of his cane and stood to his feet. We all thought he was going to leave, but he moved into the aisle and headed straight for the painting. He stepped up on the stage, never taking his eyes off of me. He hooked his cane on his arm and took a long, slow breath. His eyes were heavy, sad. I couldn't pinpoint the source of the disappointment, but I could surely see the depth of it. Several times he reached for me like he wanted to touch me, but each time he pulled back as if I carried a deadly disease.

I was confused. He looked at each scratch, each tear, and seemed torn himself at the viewing. He looked at me so tenderly I felt his touch, even though his hands never left his side. His eyes held me, and I welcomed the embrace.

He took one more step toward me, and with his face inches from mine he said for only the two of us to hear,

"I'm sorry—I just can't take you in this condition." A tear ran down his cheek. He took the cane from his arm, turned, and started walking back down the aisle.

"OK," Vito jumped in, scanning the faces in the crowd. "So, if der's no further bidding, then, thirteen hundred dollars going once, going twice . . ."

The Artist wheeled on his heal and in a urgent voice almost yelled, "Take my son!"

The room filled with question marks.

"Excuse me?" said Vito, completely confused.

"My son. I'd—I'd like to bid—my son."

Vito, still trying to track with him, asked, "For da painting?"

A young man from the back of the room stood and walked down the aisle. As he approached the Artist, he looked him confidently in the eye and said, "I'm here, Father." The Artist, chin quivering with emotion, just nodded at him, placing a hand on his shoulder as he walked by. Then the son stepped up on the stage and approached me. I saw the resemblance immediately. His eyes were those of his father.

For the first time I noticed he had an oval painter's pallet in his left hand. It was swabbed with colors of every hue. He leaned back for an instant, analyzing my condi-

tion. Then, having no brush, he dipped his fingers into several colors on the pallet. Vito and the crowd were all so taken aback by the unusual circumstances that no one even considered trying to stop him.

He leaned forward and touched his paint-covered finger to one of my scratches. Then the strangest thing happened. I felt it leave. The scratch—it was gone. He placed his pigment-drenched hand where I was torn. I felt it mend. It was healed. Stroke after stroke he made new what had been distorted; he made beautiful what had been disfigured. I was becoming, again, what the Artist had envisioned.

Then I noticed something else, equally peculiar. With each stroke of his hand, not only the paint left him for me, but part of who he was also was given in the process. His very nature was being donated with each stroke. It was as if he was willingly being absorbed for the sake of the restoration.

As he worked, I watched his eyes. He was on a mission, hellbent. He never looked away, he never looked down, but as he worked his face became more and more drawn. His very lifeblood seemed to diminish with each application. As my color improved, his worsened. The Artist had turned away, no longer able to watch as his son poured himself out into the painting.

He worked on. He depleted himself, forgiving my frayed edges. He spent his soul healing my holes. Finally, with one last sacrificial effort, he threw himself at the largest tear in my canvas and, himself, became the actual fiber of my restoration.

With that, he was gone.

It was finished. The bid accepted, the cost high.

The warehouse walls held their breath. Hundreds of hearts pounded silently like gavels into pillows. Vito gripped the podium, steadying himself from the power of the moment.

The shoulders of the Artist heaved as he sobbed. Still looking away, he hadn't witnessed any of the process, yet he seemed to have personally felt the magnitude of each stroke. Now he turned. He faced me. He took his handkerchief from his pocket and wiped his eyes. He looked again.

Now, he saw me, but not like before. This was different. I was different. There were no more rips or scratches or tears. There were no more flaws. No frays. No holes. And my colors? They were as brilliant and true as the day the Artist had touched his brush to canvas. He smiled at me. Not a smile of happiness, but one of deeper joy that has weathered a horrible pain.

He stepped to the edge of the stage.

Slowly he reached out his hand to me and said, "Come."

I did. I stepped out of the painting and into life. There was a new heart in my chest, fresh wind in my lungs. The portrait had been given life.

He took my hand and led me down the aisle. The questions of the crowd went unspoken. We got halfway to the back when the Artist turned and looked over his shoulder toward the front. I followed his eyes to see what he was looking at.

There, framed and hanging on my easel, was a portrait of his son. It was smudged, scratched, and torn. It had rips and tears and holes. Frayed. Battered, worn—lifeless.

The Artist said nothing.

The auction was over.

The bid had been very high.

As we stepped through the door into the street I felt the warm evening sunlight on my skin. With his hand gripping mine, I knew without a doubt that I was the painting—his masterpiece.

The Fire Factory

"Hey, Gabe. Check this out." A dumbstruck Michael handed the unusual work order over to his partner. It was several reams' worth of specs and diagrams. Endless equations and calculations. This was mind-boggling, even for Gabe and Michael, and these two were the very brightest bulbs at the Fire Factory.

"Have you checked upstairs with management?" asked Michael. "This can't be right. It's gotta be a mistake. We've never had an order like this before." He was right. This was big. Bigger than big. This was unprecedented, monumental.

"Who gave this to you?"

"The Chief did. He handed it to me himself." They both went back to staring at it.

The Fire Factory had been in existence for eons. It had designed, produced, and delivered a galactic array of combustibles. If it burned, the Factory could build it. Michael and Gabe had been running the place for as long as they could remember, and the Chief had never placed an order that they hadn't been able to deliver, on spec and on time. But this . . .

"I don't even know what to call this," said Gabe. "What is it?"

Michael shook his head. "I don't know, but the blueprints are clear, the Chief ordered it, so, I guess we better build it. Right?"

Gabe nodded. They put it on the docket, scheduled it for rollout a week from Monday.

The day they started working on the order, the Chief paid a visit to the Fire Factory. This was not a typical occurrence. The Chief was a busy guy. If he showed up, it meant something big was going down and he wanted to be there to give the initial spark to the project—a sort of pep talk to the troops. He stood on the overlook, leaning against the railing a hundred feet above the concrete floor of the busy factory. The shuffle and buzz of the plant diminished to a subdued hum. Machines idled. He began.

"Good morning." He looked around the cavernous

factory. There were thousands of workers—some standing, leaning on one hip, some holding on to a railing, but all bent toward the Chief, listening for every word and the meaning behind it.

"We're undertaking a great task today, one greater than we've ever undertaken before. This isn't about physics. This isn't about cosmic manipulation. This isn't about luminescence or BTUs. Today we will endeavor to fulfill the original purpose for which the Fire Factory was built."

He paused and looked around and gave a smile to Gabe and Michael, then he continued. "I have placed an order for a fire that is unique. This fire will be more than just light, more than just warmth and heat, more than just a life-giving source of nutrients for plants and creatures. It will be more than just beauty. This must be a fire like no fire that has ever burned."

Welders, engineers, and technicians all looked at each other, wondering what sort of inferno the Chief was proposing. He raised his arms and fired a challenge that ricocheted off the back wall of the factory.

"Build a fire for me," he said, "that will burn hopelessness into ashes."

"Build a fire for me," he said, "that will swallow evil whole and disown it."

"Build a fire for me," he said, "that will melt judgment into mercy."

"And build a fire for me," he concluded, "that will consume death—once and for all."

Silence. There was no applause, no cheering. He turned and walked silently through the door. Then, slowly, one by one, the workers turned and went back to work, now, with a white-hot resolve to build this . . . this supernatural fire.

The task was begun. Ignition experts laid the plans for an irrepressible fusion of infinitely combustible fibers. Molecular engineers went to work on the atomic acceleration module to be housed in a pure, microscopic environment. Biologists began calculating DNA, and microbiologists began incubating cells that could contain both living matter and atomic potential. All departments were challenged with the precarious melding of the infinite with the finite—encasing immortality within a fragile, paper-thin shell of mortality.

The thought and planning that had gone into this order were staggering in themselves, but the thing that really impressed the workers of the factory was the tenderness of heart that compelled the Chief to prepare this fire. You've got to remember, this order was going to a polluted planet; it was going to a people who had made a

sport of extinguishing fire. They had become callously proficient at stomping on sparks. There was precious little fire anywhere on this aberrant little planet. This new fire held the only hope for the salvation of this particular race. They were a species dangerously close to being swallowed in darkness. Yet, for the most part, they didn't even recognize their need for fire.

Still, the order stood.

"Remember the sun?" quipped Michael after a long day of mental exertion. "We thought that was a big deal. This makes that look like coaxing fire from gasoline."

"Yeah," replied Gabe, "plus we didn't have to disguise that fire as something small and weak. The Chief let us make it as big as we wanted. This, this is something else altogether."

This fire was different. They were accustomed to constructing highly efficient formulas for flames that burned hot and clean. Like stars, for example; they burn brilliantly in rarefied air, fueled by cosmic gases. That kind of fire naturally burns hot and clean—and pure. But this was different. This fire was intended to burn the seamiest refuse of a trash-producing species. The fuel was garbage. How do you make a fire like that burn hot and clean, let alone pure? Then tack on the added complication of condensing

it into something small and inconspicuous. Something vulnerable, fragile. This was a daunting task, and things had begun to smolder.

They worked and worked but could not get the fire to perform according to design. As soon as the core potential was reached, they found that the container was incapable of withstanding the heat. Yet, if they scaled back the capacity of the core, the power was insufficient to achieve its purpose.

Michael and Gabe pored over the schematics, checking and rechecking. They scrutinized and analyzed every factor they had figured. They brought in auditors, quality-control agents, consultants, and experts. They rethought, reran, rerouted, and rebooted. Still, no supernatural fire. They had followed every squiggle of the Chief's blueprint with a bulldogged thoroughness, yet the fire was still erratic; its purpose still compromised. What was missing? Where had they gone wrong?

That was the day the Chief showed up again, unexpectedly.

"What's the problem, guys, fire go out?" he asked lightheartedly.

Gabe and Michael weren't exactly in a joking mood. "This, this . . . fire you've ordered," Michael said. "We've done everything the plans show, everything. We've checked

and rechecked." Then, more tentatively, "Is it possible, sir, that—something has been—left out of the equation? We've tried, Chief, but this thing is killin' us."

The Chief looked at Michael like he'd been expecting this moment to arrive.

"I knew this fire would require everything from you guys. You always put yourselves fully into my projects. The difference is, this one's going to require everything from me as well. This one's likely to kill me too." He looked half-serious when he said it. He continued, "The birth of this fire will be our greatest moment. Nothing will be the same from here on out." He smiled at Gabe and said, "Here's what I want you to do."

He placed both of his hands over the plans and stared into the pages. Then, with a slight tremble in his voice he said, "Put me in the fire."

This, Gabe and Michael were not expecting. They looked at each other, wondering whether the Chief was feeling OK. Gabe spoke first.

"Listen, Chief, give us a few more days. Maybe we missed something in the equation. Maybe we forgot some obscure detail. We can make this work."

Michael continued, "Yeah, Chief, give us some more time. We can't put you in the fire . . . that's, that's crazy."

"I know," he said. "Put me in the fire."

"But, sir, you know these people. They're dangerous. They put out fires. They . . . they hate fire."

"I know. Put me in the fire."

"But, Chief, this is—this is suicidal."

He put his hand on Michael's shoulder reassuringly and said, "It'll be OK. There are some fires that can't be put out . . . not for long anyhow. A spark will rise out of the ashes. Trust me."

We retooled. We fired up the ovens again. We had a new recipe. Now, with our secret ingredient, we could factor in the physics of forgiveness, the unexplainable geothermics of grace, the algebraic logarithms of limitless love.

We put him in the fire . . . and it worked. It burned like no fire had ever burned before. The core sizzled with eternal potential, yet it looked completely harmless, cradled in helpless humanity.

Every worker stood silently, reverently, the day we sent the spark on its journey. It blazed a swath across the sky, carried on the wings of the hopes and fears of thousands of dedicated Fire Factory workers.

It was Christmas Day in the year Zero, the day fire came to earth.

The Tomorrow Tower

I was a professional stair climber. That's what I did. Find the toughest, steepest, longest flights of stairs in the world, and climb them. Massive quads and diamond-shaped calves powered me like pistons up the most grueling stairways. I was a monster of elevation. They called me the "Stair Master," the "Up Man."

In my early days I was unstoppable. The World Trade Center, the Washington Monument, the Empire State Building—pieces of cake. I did the Sears Tower in Chicago in under 13 minutes. At 2,232 steps, that's more than 2.86 steps per second. To this day, nobody has matched that feat.

The Great Wall of China? I did every step at every

entrance and ran the lengths in between. Talk about torture. ESPN did a feature story on me for that one.

I once hopped up the side of the Grand Canyon on my right foot—all the way to the top, then turned around, ran down and hopped back up using my left foot. That was pretty tough.

I don't know what it is about me, maybe it's genetic, but I always want to be at the top, and to be there first. I don't take direction very well and I never accept defeat. I guess I'm as stubborn as I am strong. Some people say I have control issues. Some say I have an altitude complex. I don't know about that, all I know is that climbing gave reason to my existence, so I dedicated my life to perfecting it.

I ate right, I slept right. I trained like a madman, all to attain my goal of climbing the steepest and the tallest.

And speaking of the steepest and the tallest, let's talk about the real deal. The mother of all climbs. This was no skyscraper, no little two-bit canyon. Those were just warmup events compared to this—like a 5K run to a marathoner. Everybody knows there's only one climb that can mark your career. Only one climb against which you can really measure yourself. This one has the potential to make Olympic gods look dreadfully human. This tower rises and disappears into the clouds. Rumor has it that

there is no top to this tower, as no one has ever seen it. Even on clear days the rounded glass exterior just dissolves into the sky, making its peak nebulous at best. This massive structure makes the Sears tower look like a Kmart. Imagine the Eiffel Tower on steroids and you've got . . .

The Tomorrow Tower.

To a certain extent the Tomorrow Tower represented my existence, the culmination of my career, my life. Every moment of my past led me to the foot of this tower; every climb, merely preparation for scaling Tomorrow's stairs. In one sense, this tower was so central to my being that you could say I'd been climbing it since the day I was born. Who I was and where I was going were about to be played out on the mazelike stairwells of this edifice.

The Tomorrow Tower was indescribably complex. A futuristic marvel of glass and steel. It was huge, and yet it had no rooms. It was a vertical wonder and yet it had no elevators, no escalators; only an elaborate network of open stairways reaching like fingers toward the sky. The tower seemed to have been designed for the sole experience of transition, the journey from here to there. Just walking through the doors gave you the impression that you were embarking on a pilgrimage.

In a sense, Tomorrow was more than a mere tower. It

seemed to have an identity, a personality all its own. It washed mystically over all who entered, like a surreal divine breath. People actually believed that it reached so high that it could take you into tomorrow. Of course, you first had to climb.

It started simply, one stairwell, one step. I began slowly, wanting to pace myself for this ultramarathon. It felt good to finally be on my way, climbing. The first flight reached a point where it branched out into two stairways. Since everything was going up, I didn't give too much thought as to which way I went. I just kept pumping my legs.

As the maze of stairwells grew more complex they grew increasingly more beautiful. There were stairs made of polished mahogany, copper, abalone, and turquoise. Stairs made of marbled oak with inlayed ivory. Hand-placed fieldstone stairs led to a glass spiral staircase injected with azure-colored water, each flight supported only by the previous flight. No pillars, no cables, no visible support system. The design was both brilliant and beautiful.

Through the first fifteen hundred stairs my pace held steady, my heart rate was good. Tomorrow was looking doable, I was confident.

As the particular stairway I was on passed closer to the atrium of the tower, I noticed a very interesting sight.

There, at the heart of Tomorrow, reaching from the ground straight up to the heavens, was what I can only describe as a glowing stream of pure water, which appeared to be flowing contrary to gravity, being pulled along by a gentle breeze. It was weird, a combination of wind, water, and light, intertwined and married in a way that I had never witnessed before. I could see they were separate entities, and yet they were almost indistinguishable from each other, part of a whole.

I didn't think too much of it at the time because I had a job to do. There was Tomorrow to conquer. I climbed on.

I'm not sure if the stairs got steeper or if I was just tiring. I knew I was slowing. As I came to choices in direction, I started choosing stairwells that took me closer to the outside wall, hoping the view of the world below would motivate me, reenergize me.

It didn't work. Fatigue kept on coming. I started feeling that burn in my quads. The lactic acid was building up. My aerobic endurance was stalling. The training regimen I had followed so religiously was starting to fall short. The challenge of Tomorrow was turning out to be more than my equal.

Now the stairs were rising two, even three feet at a time. The steady cadence had become labored, irregular. I wasn't

really noticing the beauty anymore, the effort was too demanding. It was all I could do to keep putting one foot in front of the other.

After one particularly grueling flight I abruptly came to a dead end. I almost stepped over the edge. It was miles to the bottom. There were no options on this stairwell, it just flat-out ended. I climbed back down and took another path. This one was even steeper than the last. Not only were these stairs four feet high, but they were only inches deep. The footing was shaky. This was turning into an Everest.

As I pulled myself up one more step, I found myself again perched on a narrow ledge, teetering on the top of another dead-end column. The tower still soared above me, but this stairway, like the other one, just ran out of steps. I was getting scared. Thoughts of record-breaking climbs were distant dreams now. Just finishing in one piece was all I was praying for.

The sweat was stinging my eyes; my knees were scraped and bleeding. I could barely feel my feet. I followed more stairs to more dead ends, more climbs to more nothingness. I was getting panicky. Everywhere seemed to lead only to nowhere. I leaned forward, hands on my knees, panting. I walked down and came back up the same steps again, hoping reality would change. It didn't. The top step

was still the top step. There was no resolution, no reprieve, no going on. There was no next step. The air was thin. I needed oxygen, water. My heart was redlining. I was lost, exhausted, dehydrated.

I sat down in a puddle of sweat and confusion. Demoralized by endless climbing and never reaching a satisfying destination, I collapsed. I gave up. I quit. This was a horribly new experience for me. A first. Succumbing to anyone or anything was completely contrary to my nature, a foreign concept. The taste of my own limitations stuck to the roof of my mouth. I was choking, not so much on my failure, but on my newly acquired understanding that my failure was inevitable. As I hung my head between my knees, I saw the shallow shadow of my own humanity. It was humbling.

The Tomorrow Tower had delivered its message loud and clear: "Who you are is not enough."

I couldn't hold in the disappointment anymore. I did something else that was new to me; I started crying. The questions slid from my lungs as I sobbed. "There's gotta be more than this. Where is Tomorrow? Does it exist? This can't be all there is. Please, I need help." I heard the words dripping down the stairway, trailing off into silence.

I still couldn't breathe. I felt deathly chilled. My mouth

was parched, my eyes fuzzy. I remember thinking, *This is it. I'm not gonna make it through today.* I felt myself starting to pass out. I squeezed my eyes shut and laid my head down on the stairs. Physically I've hit the wall before, but this was different. My spirit and soul had crashed too.

That's when I felt it. A slight breeze ruffled my hair. Several droplets of water splashed against my cheek. I felt this warming glow wrap around me, seeping deeply into my body. Still with my head on the stair, I opened my eyes and struggled to focus. I couldn't believe what I saw. The fountain at the center of the tower had left its path and was bending toward me. It had altered its course and almost appeared to be reaching out to me. It kept coming and coming, until it came to within two feet of me, then it slowed and stopped.

It almost seemed like it was looking at me, empathizing with my condition, inviting me into itself. Now, only inches away, I saw its beauty. It became clear to me that this fountain contained everything I lacked. It offered everything I needed. It was everything I wasn't. In an unspoken language, the fountain seemed to be saying to me, "Trust me, I'm enough."

I squinted, looking deeper into the fountain. I thought I saw something. I did. A sight that forever changed me.

There, in the wind and water and light, was tomorrow. It wasn't above, it was within.

I lunged for the fountain, wrapping my arms around its cool stream. The pure water washed over me, cleansing me, refreshing me. The breeze entered my lungs, resuscitating me, indwelling and saturating my whole being. The light melted the deathly chill that had held me in its frigid grip.

My eyes cleared. I stood; revived, renewed. With one final splash, glimmer, and gust, the fountain returned to its course, once again standing regally at the heart of Tomorrow.

Now, instead of it bending toward me, I chose to bend toward it. I found stairs that kept me in close proximity to this supernatural phenomenon. I realized that the fountain was more than just an architectural ornament, it was the very essence of the Tomorrow Tower. In a sense, it was the elevator, the way.

Now, with the aid of the light, dead ends began sprouting with throughways. Now I was finding paths through the heart of the hardest climbs, ways I had never seen before. The climbing was still tough, but now I had direction. I wasn't just randomly striving.

I climbed on.

People still call me the "Up Man," but my ascent would

have long been over were it not for the fountain at the heart of Tomorrow. It saved my life. I can't explain this fountain, but I've experienced it. I don't understand it, but I know it's real.

I've learned that stairs shadowed from the light were never meant to be climbed. The best paths are always within an arm's reach of the water. The breeze only blows on the way that's true.

It's been years now, and I'm still climbing. Ya know, maybe the rumor is true, maybe there is no top to Tomorrow. What if it goes on forever? I'm thinking I'll get there someday, but for now, today, I'm just following this incredible fountain on my journey up.

Red Kite,
Blue Kite

It was the springtime of their youth, the time when the fancy of all young kites drifts to thoughts of soaring at oxygen-deprived altitudes. Skimming the tips of outstretched oaks, surveying endless acres of freshly tilled earth, and witnessing panoramic views spiked with small-town church steeples. Ah, spring . . . when every breeze beckons and every fluffy cloud becomes a fantasized destination of choice.

It was a good time to be a kite.

Every kite, more than anything else, desires to fly. Even before they understand the concept of flight, they yearn for it. It's the unknown entity they subconsciously crave,

the missing puzzle piece that, when experienced, is the natural fulfillment of their existence.

Today, the KiteMaster held two kites in his hands as he headed to the open field. This would be their virgin voyage, their first time to experience negative G's—gravity in reverse. The pair quivered with anticipation.

They were a couple of average-looking kites, alike in many ways. Each was airworthy, each capable of flight—built for it. But they also had their differences, their own wrinkles, bends, and curves. They talked a little differently when the wind was rattling their skin. Their nylon tails carried their own statements of style, but other than that, there wasn't much that separated them. After all, they were both kites.

One red, one blue.

The KiteMaster had fashioned each of these kites with his own hand. All of his kites were his own creations. No kits in his collection. No punch-out prefab flyers in his fleet. Every one was a handcrafted original. He chose the materials himself, cut the wood, fashioned the spars, and painted the paper sails. He trimmed, treated, tucked, and tied everything to his exact specifications. He glued the sail around the string and pulled it tight along the leading edges. He knotted the bridle with a stronger line, and calculated the

perfect angle of loft. Each kite was reduced of excess weight till it was a mere breath away from slipping the grasp of gravity. When he had finished the red and blue kites, he had looked at them admiringly and said, "These are very good."

Having reached a broad meadow, the KiteMaster picked up the red kite and without warning tossed it skyward, running headlong into the wind, granting flight to the little red dirigible. Instantly the red flyer was changed, free from the constraints of earth, soaring at breakneck speed straight toward heaven. One minute mortal, the next, eternal. First bound, then free.

That first flight was both exhilarating and brutal. The wind rushing across the red sail was breathtaking—a wide-eyed blend of danger and daring. His paper flapped furiously as the northeasterly gales tested the mettle of his wood. Erratic leaps of altitude made the red kite's stomach somersault as the KiteMaster yanked on the line, constantly pulling—pulling his red body back into the teeth of the wind. Always, ever facing the Master.

That first flight may not have been pretty, but the little red-headed glider was hooked. A convert. A believer. Every other experience of his short life smacked of tedium and triviality compared to grabbing air at elevations he'd only

dreamed of. This was living! This was what he was made to do—to be. He was certain of it. His search for meaning and purpose was over.

The blue kite was next. He flew even higher, farther, and longer. The wind swished through his tail and crackled his paper. The blue kite screamed with pleasure as he danced from cloud to cloud till the sun's music faded. The thrill left his wooden bones tingling for hours.

That night, in the garage, they stayed up well into the evening, reliving every last spiral and arc of their sorties. As they drifted off, they determined to be eagerly waiting by the garage door in the morning. They would be poised and ready, begging if need be, to go flying.

The next day the KiteMaster arrived bright and early with miles of string in his hands and an eager invitation, "Who wants to fly?" The red and blue kites were stumbling over one another to be first in line, craving the spiritual aphrodisiac of flight.

They flew every day for weeks, months, challenging the sky to duels. They played follow the leader with every willing swallow, shadow tag with every consenting hawk.

The red kite never seemed to tire of flying—of spending time with the KiteMaster. He loved catching the full breath of the wind and feeling that firm, steady pull, anchored to

the strong hand of the Master. Though tethered by a string, he was given free run of the sky . . . to swoop, to soar, to dive, to pirouette. Not constrained, but guided.

The red kite soon learned not to fight the finessing touch of the KiteMaster. Each flight was a tutorial in breez-ology, every afternoon a primer in airstream management. With each hour spent with the Master in training, the red kite learned more about the aerodynamics of life . . . what it took to stay aloft and how to weather the differing winds and currents. He learned how to rely and rest on the KiteMaster's line when the howling north wind blew, and he learned to accept the slack when a warm southerly wind carried and sustained him.

He soon could recognize even the hint of a suggestion from the KiteMaster. The way the string laid across the Master's fingertips carried surprising significance—nudged to the left, caressed to the right, sometimes held loosely, sometimes firmly with unswerving certitude. Even the slightest move spoke volumes to the red kite. It was unmis-takable . . . the gentle voice of Houston to his orbiting child.

As time went on, the red kite realized that the real thrill was not found in the flight, but in being flown by the KiteMaster.

The blue kite, however, had begun to drift. Somehow he

got it into his head that he was virtually capable of flight on his own, that he didn't really need the KiteMaster at all. Maybe some other flier could take him up, someone who wouldn't tug and pull so much, someone who would allow him to do his own thing, go his own way. The KiteMaster had too many suggestions, as if there was a right and wrong way to fly.

The blue kite cruised the sky with one flier after another, never finding one who could fly him without strings attached. After dozens of uninspiring flights, the blue kite grew apathetic about the sky. It had become ordinary, average, predictable.

Soon, the blue kite gave up on flight altogether. He chose to stay in the garage. He decided that if flight was no longer going to be fulfilling, why bother with it. He'd pour his energies into something else.

He started collecting kite ornaments, pretty little things to hang on his tail. Shiny, spangly, dangly things that looked good, but were a definite detriment to airworthiness. On the rare occasion he chose to fly, the added weight of his accessorized tail limited his elevation, holding him closer to earth. The more he wore, the harder it was to get airborne. Too many shiny treasures, and it was almost an impossibility for him to taste heaven.

The blue kite wasn't happy. He had a pretty good idea where he and happiness had parted company, but finding his way back was not so easy. After all, he was a proud kite.

One day the red kite shimmied over to the blue kite's box. He had missed talking with the blue kite. They had been the best of friends, like brothers—born on the very same day, learned to fly the same day. Now they hadn't spoken for several years. They were both a little more weathered, a little more creased, but still friends.

"Remember how we talked till all hours of the morning after our first flight?" said the red kite. "What a day that was!"

The blue kite hadn't thought about that day for ages. It had been a great day. He had been dead sure that life would never be the same after that. Life suddenly had wings.

What happened to that hope? he thought. *How did I get sidetracked from that thrill? Nobody has ever flown me like the Master. Nobody has cared about me like that.*

Just seeing the red kite again made him long to be held, to be tossed into the breeze by the Master. *But surely the KiteMaster wouldn't fly me again,* he thought. *If only I could go back and do it all over again.*

The red kite, seeing his fear and anticipation, said, "Come on. The KiteMaster misses you as much as you miss him. He'll fly you. I know he will."

Just then the garage door opened. It was like the Master had been waiting just outside the door, hoping to be invited in.

The blue kite looked at him, shame causing his paper sail to hang heavily on his frame. His string was in tangles, his bridle in knots. Years of loneliness and failure welled up inside him.

The KiteMaster, seeing only through eyes of forgiveness, knelt down beside the blue kite. He took the worldworn kite in his hands, ever so slowly and gently. He brushed the dust from the blue kite and rubbed a deep crease from his wrinkled sail. Then—he just held him—tenderly, in a cleansing silence.

With the blue kite's consent, the KiteMaster lovingly untied each ornament from his tail and placed it in a box. As the kite was freed from each shiny anchor, his bones began to dance in the breeze. The snap of his paper sail sent shivers up his spine. The memory of flight began bubbling in him.

He was coming back to life.

Finally the KiteMaster looked at the blue kite and with an assuring smile said, "You know, it's a perfect day for flying. What do you say we go shake up the sky . . . take a peek at heaven?"

The blue kite didn't need to be asked twice. Then, as if launched from a rocket pad, the KiteMaster dashed out the garage door, making a beeline for the field, towing the blue kite behind him. The blue kite held on to the string with all his might. Before they had even reached the edge of the field the blue kite was airborne—not just flying, but being flown. Dipping and diving in total synchronicity, flawlessly orchestrated by the maestro of flight.

It was spring again, in more ways than one. And yes, it surely was a good time to be a kite.

True North

I was sitting, staring through the computer screen one night. I wasn't looking *at* it but *past* it, like it was one of those 3-D Magic Eye posters. I was enjoying this moment of dreamlike vegetation when suddenly, right before my unfocused eyes, my computer screen went ballistic, bonkers, berserk—and morphed into a 3-D virtual-reality cyberspace. I was sucked into the monitor like it was a giant 100,000-watt Hoover and spit out into a vast, black nothingness. There I saw my life magnetically suspended between two poles, free-floating in cyberspace.

One pole looked like a vast city. Neon signs everywhere, like Vegas at night. A 24/7 party. The place was jammin'. Music screaming down every alley, money flying from fist to

fist, and street vendors on every corner hawking everything from faux peace to imitation happiness.

From their six square feet of paved real estate they were barking,

Slightly used purpose here!
Get your daily dose of meaning!
Self-fulfillment, like new, only two bucks!

From a distance, where my life was hanging, the city of neon looked pretty good. The magnetic pull was strong. I knew that an ounce of apathy on my part would have guaranteed my residence in the Neon City, and part of me would feel very "at home" there.

Yet, one thing kind of gave me the creeps about this place. There was a rumor I'd heard. It went like this: "If you spend your life in the Neon City, it becomes who you are. And there's this black hole, waiting, just past the outskirts of town. They say it sneaks up on you. Quite often, by the time you realize you're headed for it, it's too late. Lost in cyberspace forever."

Well, when I turned to check out the other pole, it took a while for my eyes to adjust from the barrage of neon to a far less frenetic sight. A city of boulevards and lakes.

More green than neon. Interestingly, it appeared to be perpetually bathed in natural light. The water tower simply read, "True North."

They say the mayor of True North is an interesting guy. Honest to a fault. The kind of guy who'd die for you. There was a strong pull here, too, but it appeared to be much more subtle. Not seducing, but welcoming. It kind of made me feel like I wouldn't have lived if I hadn't at least driven the boulevards or taken a walk around one of its lakes.

Not many people leave True North. I guess it's a pretty great place to live. But a lot of people live just outside the city limits, although I'm not quite sure why. I mean, it's so beautiful and peaceful inside. Maybe they just want to be far enough out so they can see the lights of the Neon City every once in a while—maybe make a quick trip there and back.

Seems like more and more people are leaving the Neon City, though, and migrating north. I guess the tourism brochure for the Neon City overstates its quality of life. And . . . it's not exactly a secret that their mayor's a real snake.

As I observed these two cities I realized something. True North is the kind of place I've been looking for my whole life. People aren't perfect there, but they are honest, truthful, and kind. I know I'd have great friends there. But yet

this fascination I felt for the Neon City seemed almost overpowering. Its magnets must be pointed right at me.

Well, as I was floating there, being pulled in two different directions, all of a sudden I get this Instant Message—and get this, it's from the mayor of True North. This is too weird! He says he wants to adopt me, like I'd be his son. Said he wants me to move in with him, right in the mayor's residence.

Whoa. This whole thing was making me a little uncomfortable. I mean, I don't even know this guy, and he wants to adopt me? Who is he anyhow? Then he sends this message: "I know this sounds crazy, but I've been looking for you forever. You've been floating out there so long. I've got a place here that is so right for you. You could have your own room. We could hang out, get to know each other better." Then, almost like he was laughing, he said, "Sure, it's not heaven, but you can almost see it from here."

Well, I entered my response to him, saying how much I appreciated the offer but I thought maybe I'd just move a little closer. "Besides," I said, "I wouldn't be a very good roommate. My life isn't very neat. I've got a lot of garbage that I haven't taken care of. So maybe I'll just move to the suburbs for a while, see how I like it." And as I punched those words into the keyboard, I caught a glimpse over my shoulder of the Neon City.

I swear, this guy is omniscient or something because these words flew onto my screen: "It's not real, Joe. There's nothing there for you. It's all a smoke screen. Pretend happiness, temporary significance, purpose with a dead end. It's self-destructive. Oh yeah, one last thing. If you're gonna make a move, remember the Realtors' Rule, 'Location is everything!' You can move to the suburbs, the projects outside of True North, but why? I IM'd you because I want you to have life, abundant life . . . real joy, deep peace, lasting contentment, meaning, purpose."

He continued, "I know you're not perfect. I'm not going to disown you when you mess up. I'm kind of expecting you to. I don't want you because you're perfect, I want you because I love you. If you move in, I know some of that stuff you're not proud of is going to disappear. And when that stuff goes, the Neon City won't have such a strong pull on you anymore."

Well, you're probably wondering, What happened? It took a while, but I got rid of a few ugly things that were cluttering up my life. Excess baggage—the things that seemed more at home under artificial lighting. I've adopted this new motto; well, it's new for me anyhow. It came from a two-thousand-year-old e-mail sent to these Philippian people. It says, "I consider everything a loss,

compared to the surpassing greatness of knowing the mayor of True North."

I'm living next door to the mayor now. Over the last few years I keep moving closer and closer. I'm spending more and more time with him. We've gotten to be quite close. I wish I could say I was living in the mayor's residence, but that would be a lie. Someday.

Last week the mayor was telling me about a place where there's this whole other reality. A place past True North. It sounded great. He says it's out of this world—unbelievably cool! It wouldn't surprise me if he's already been there. And he said everybody who's ever lived in True North, well, they retire there, permanently. It's like the Florida of cyberspace. Sounds like heaven to me!

CAUTION

If you haven't already done so, may I suggest you flip the book over and read your way back to the middle. Reading "Home" now may cause slight discoloration. And we don't want that.

So . . . save "Home" for last.